D0361715

Remember the Holocaust

# Remember
## *the*
# Holocaust

&

## *A memoir of survival*

by Helen Farkas

FITHIAN PRESS / SANTA BARBARA / 1995

Published by Fithian Press
A division of Daniel and Daniel, Publishers, Inc.
Post Office Box 1525
Santa Barbara, CA 93102

Design by Eric Larson

LIBRARY OF CONGRESS CATALOGING-IN-PUBLICATION DATA
Farkas, Helen
    Remember the Holocaust : a memoir of survival / Helen Farkas.
       p.   cm.
    ISBN 1-56474-125-7
    1. Farkas, Helen. 2. Holocaust, Jewish, (1939–1945)—Personal
narratives. 3. Holocaust survivors—Biography.
    I. Title.
D804.F36  1995
940.53'18'092—dc20
   [B]                       94-33684
                               CIP

*Dedicated to my family:*
*past, present, and future*

I wish to thank my daughter, Amber Farkas, for her help in putting together the manuscript for this book, and my granddaughter, Kailei Ritcheson, for inspiring me to write my story of the Holocaust so that it would never be forgotten.

I would also like to thank my grandnephew, Chaim Eyal, Ph.D. (Irene's son), for his help in preparing the manuscript for publication.

Special gratitude goes to my husband, Joe, who has comforted me through fifty years of memories and nightmares.

# Contents

*A section of photographs begins on page 85*

# Remember the Holocaust

# CHAPTER 1

# Preceding the Holocaust

My name is Helen Farkas. I was born in Romania in a city called Satu-Mare. It was a city of approximately 100,000 people at that time. In 1918, before I was born, Satu-Mare (in the province of Transylvania) was within the borders of Hungary. It became a part of Romania after the First World War.

I was born in 1920 to Freida and Chaim Safar. My parents had a total of nine children. In order, from the oldest to the youngest, we were Moshe, Miriam, Eddie, Lenke, Regina, Ethel, myself, Nathan, and Andor. We had a comfortable life in a large house with a vegetable garden and a fruit orchard in the yard. My parents' hobby was tending the garden. My father was a shoemaker, and my mother was a busy housewife raising nine children in a time when there were no luxuries such as refrigerators, cars, washing machines, supermarkets, and other conveniences that we take for granted today. My parents worked hard to raise us as good and moral people and provided us with a good education for those days. I remember life as being good with the simple pleasures of life—playing games, doing sports, swimming, reading and being with other members of our family.

We did not have high expectations of life and we found

the simple things to be satisfying. Our futures were to be based on the ethics of hard work, good family and friends. As the older children came of age, some of them married and moved to different towns to raise their own families. Miriam moved to Kolosvar. Regina moved to Gherla (which is close to Kolosvar) where she gave birth to three children. By 1944 all my siblings were married except Nathan and Andor. I was not married either, and my brother Andor and I were still living at home with our parents. Nathan, however, had left for Budapest with false papers given to him by a non-Jewish friend.

At that time I was engaged to marry Joe Farkas, who is my present husband. Joe was the center-forward player on a local soccer team, and a big star. Soccer was the most popular sport, and almost everyone was interested in following it, just like football or basketball in the U.S. today. Joe was very handsome, and we were very much in love. We used to go to the grape arbor in the back of my home and nibble on the grapes, talk about our future, and kiss in the shade and solitude that we found there.

Religion was part of our lifestyle. Our household was kept kosher, we followed the Jewish laws and traditions regularly and celebrated the holidays around the calendar. However, religion was not an overwhelming or burdensome part of our existence. It was a natural part of our daily lives. We were raised as Jews, we attended the synagogue on occasion but, as was the case in most Jewish families, the males, my father and my brothers, were the ones most involved with religious practice and worship. The girls did not have to take religious matters too seriously, other than carrying out the most common traditions. In Satu-Mare about one-third of the population was Jewish. We were very well integrated with our non-Jewish neighbors, friends and their children. We did not intermarry, but we had friendships that lasted from childhood until the holocaust began. In those days, typically, people were born in their family-owned houses and grew into adulthood as neighbors. People did not move around or relocate as frequently as they do today. Everyone knew everyone else. Friends, whether Jewish or non-Jewish, would often remain friends for life. With the war, however, many friendships had changed, typically because of the fears and threats brought about by the war and the Nazi regime.

During the times preceding the holocaust, we had a good life without any significant racial problems. There were, however, incidents of discrimination and prejudice that signified the coming changes. For example, gentile parents who had to discipline a child would sometimes say, "Watch out, or I'll call the Jew." But we were used to this usage, and it did not bother us. Except for this sort of reference, we were not persecuted. We knew that discrimination and persecution existed, but we were good neighbors and we perceived out neighbors as equals and equally good.

At the time, we lived in Transylvania, near the Hungarian border. On the fifth of September, 1940, the Hungarians took this area over, upon orders from Germany, as Hitler had given Transylvania back to them. Suddenly we became Hungarian residents. It was after this event that the persecution of the Jews began. First we started reading in the daily paper about new government orders stating specifically what Jews may or may not do. Little by little our freedom became restricted. Jewish doctors and lawyers could no longer practice their professions, people holding government positions suddenly lost their jobs, and so on.

Every day there would be a new bulletin in the town newspaper instructing us about what had to be done in compliance with the new rules and restrictions. One day it was announced that we must turn in our radios (without being financially reimbursed, of course, although the authorities did issue us a small paper note, as a receipt!). They obviously did not want us to know what was going on in the world. At that time, a radio was a very valuable possession. My brother Andor, who was then nineteen years old, owned a small radio (which was even more valuable than the large ones). He did not want to surrender it, so he took a chance and kept it.

Our home was in the suburbs, and my family tried to build a bunker in our backyard. The neighbors, however, discovered it and we were compelled to abandon the project for fear of negative consequences. My father used to go down into the basement to listen to the radio. He used a length of wire for an antenna in order to receive the Voice of America program. He knew some English because he had lived in America for four years before the First World War. He used to come up from the basement and tell us disturbing and terrible news, for example, that thousands of Jewish men, women, and children were found dead in mass graves in Poland, in Transmistria, and in Russia—places that the Germans had occupied. We thought my father was losing his mind to believe such nonsense. We simply could not conceive that this was possible in this day and age. We could conceive of men killing men in war times, but not helpless women and children. We thought that it must all be American propaganda. This was 1944, but it had all actually begun much earlier—in 1940—and had gradually gotten worse. My father started listening to outside news reports in 1942 or 1943, and we had begun to develop a fear of what was to come and anxieties about what seemed to be happening in the world.

Within just a few years, the population around us became very brainwashed by propaganda, which was disseminated mostly through radio and by the display of grotesque pictures of Jews in newspapers, magazines, and street posters. I think that many people actually believed that the Jews were a subversive element and that they were cheating the population out of their rights. Many Jews were bankers and teachers, holding intellectual and influential positions, and many people actually believed that the Jews were somehow stealing all the good things from the rest of the population and, therefore, had to be controlled. Many people were made to think that the Jews were simply being taken away, removed from the area, and they did not realize that the Jews were being exterminated. To this day I find it difficult to comprehend how the gentile population took to the Nazi propaganda so rapidly, so completely, and without question.

In about 1943 some Slovakians who had been "picked up" and who appeared to have disappeared, somehow managed to return. Apparently they had escaped. They came back with stories about atrocities and murders committed by German soldiers with the active help of the local government forces. In my experience, the Hungarians were not sympathetic at all to the cause and plight of the victims. Even our neighbors exhibited little sympathy when such atrocities first began to happen in our town. Very few of them were moved to take risks of exposing themselves to danger by helping the Jews. Most of them were just too afraid of the possible consequences or too apathetic and indifferent to the suffering around them. Many people were simply not willing to be bothered by the injustice inflicted upon us and by the mistreatment we had to endure, let alone to risk their lives on our behalf.

In around 1942, after my sister Ethel's husband, Bandi,

was taken away to the forced labor camp and was not heard from, she sub-rented half of her apartment to a young couple. They had seen the rent announcement in her window, applied, and she liked them. They moved in, and all was well for a while. The rent income helped Ethel pay her own rent. The couple spoke Hungarian with a foreign accent, and they had said that they were both professionals, working for the government. As time went on, they often quarreled in Polish, which my sister did not understand. One day, in early 1944, the police showed up and carried the man away, but the woman stayed behind. Ethel found out that they had not been married and that the woman tipped off the authorities to the fact that the man was Jewish and a foreigner. The man never returned, and Ethel managed to get rid of this woman within a few months. Many young Jewish men and women had a similar fate, as they tried to disguise their Jewish identity by living with a non-Jewish partner, as a married couple.

In the early forties, the first law against the Jews was issued, requiring all Jews to provide proof of their citizenship. Although many had been born and raised in their community for several generations, if they could not produce valid evidence of their citizenship, they were forcefully expelled. Within a very short time, many had to leave the country via Poland, which was not a harmless border crossing. Rather, there was use of brutal force and harsh treatment, which typically included torture, robbery, rape and murder. I knew of several young men and women who, through some kind of miracle, managed to escape and hide with false identification cards, posing as gentiles. They had supported themselves by working at odd jobs for Jews, and never stayed too long in one place, for fear of being discovered.

In 1943 a law that required all Jews to wear a yellow Star

of David on their left lapel went into effect. We had to sew the stars on our coats and jackets and, in fact, on every outer garment that we used for outdoor wear. Needless to say, this highly visible mark of identification brought a tremendous vulnerability into our lives and daily existence. We became the targets of hoodlums and the laughing stock of many. Understandably, we did not dare to use the sidewalks at times, for fear of getting poked in the ribs, being kicked, or being subjected to smirks and derogatory remarks such as, "Get off the sidewalk, Jew!" Many religious males, young and old, were pulled or dragged by their beards until their faces bled without provocation. Our only alternative was to stay home as much as we possibly could. We were isolated, could not go to the theater, were unable to stroll the city streets and boardwalks, nor could we visit each other. The only relief we had from this humiliation was at the riverbank, where we did not have to wear the yellow star on our bathing suits.

We, the younger members of our family, resented the new rule and rebelled quietly against the requirement to wear the yellow star. Our parents could provide no solution other than to say to us, "Don't cringe or hide in shame. The shame is on those who rule over us and make us wear this star. Pull yourself up. Hold your head up high. You have nothing to be ashamed of. You have committed no crime. You are a law-abiding person. You are who you are and you cannot change that, even if you want to. The law would not allow you to convert to another religion. Once a Jew, always a Jew. It is our destiny, as it has been for thousands of years."

With the passage of time, the laws became more and more restrictive to Jews. In 1944, just before Passover, a new law was announced, ordering all Jews to move into ghettos.

A few blocks were designated as the ghetto area. Through sheer coincidence, my sister Ethel lived in the designated ghetto area. As soon as we found out where we were being moved, we started storing food and supplies at Ethel's house, since we had no idea what was going to befall us. Shortly after Passover we were all made to move to the ghetto. Elders of our town and the synagogue, acting in official capacity, carried out the orders to move us. I presume that they were either forced to do this, or that they acted willingly, not realizing what was going to happen. In any case, it was with their help that we were eventually shipped off to Auschwitz.

At this time, Joe and I were both twenty-three years old and had been going steady for six years. We wanted to get married, but as the times were changing and since it looked as if Joe would be "recruited" to do forced labor, we did not have the opportunity to become married. We decided that it was best to wait for more stable and better times.

Many of the young Jewish men were taken to forced labor camps. They were shipped out to be used by Hungarian Nazis as human mine detectors, or at other "disposable" jobs. Joe was lucky to become a cook for their battalion. The "recruits" were not issued uniforms, but had to wear a yellow arm band on their own clothes, to designate their status.

The last time I saw Joe was shortly before we were put into the ghetto. He was already in a forced labor camp, but he managed to get away one last time to say good-bye to me and to his family. We then were separated by the war. I did not see him again until after the war was over. In the meantime, we received no news of each other, and he did not know whether I was dead or alive, and neither did I.

Following our displacement from our homes and our

relocation into the ghetto, the authorities hung up banners on Jewish homes in Budapest and in other cities, proclaiming that "The Jews of this house have been smoked out."

I have a girlfriend, Magda, who lives in Budapest, who in the early spring of 1944 sent me a letter—not by mail, but via the courier who came to Satu-Mare. Her cousin Magda wrote to me how, one day, the Hungarian "Arrow-Cross" Nazis dragged her, along with many other Jews, off the streetcars. They were marched off into the Dohany Street Synagogue, where many other Jews were gathered. From there, they were taken to other locations. She had ended up in one central concentration place, among thousands of other Jews. Many others were dragged off streetcars to the shore of the Danube River and were shot on the spot. The water turned red from blood. While grouped with the others, Magda saw many Jews being pushed into cattle rail wagons, to be shipped off to "work," so they were told. She was positioned in one of the back rows. Familiar with the surroundings, she managed to slip away and escape under the cover of darkness and make her way to a hiding place, posing as a gentile.

When we read Magda's detailed account, we could not believe that anything like this could happen to us, having lived in a rural area. We thought this could only happen in the large cities. Besides, we thought, what is wrong with being taken to work? It is still better than to be placed in ghettos. At that time, we could not fully absorb the real impact of the situation on our lives and on the lives of so many others. As a matter of fact, we had no choice. We could not have gone anywhere anyway. We were doomed.

# Chapter 2

# The Ghetto

Life in the ghetto was hard. We were given no food, and we felt lucky that we had had the foresight to stockpile some food. We had brought in whole hams that we hung in the attic. We had live chickens and geese as well. We all shared in the ghetto. I remember, for example, that after three weeks we ran out of yeast to make bread, but there were others who had some and they shared it with us. They gave us pieces of dough in which to culture the yeast so that we could bake.

We were also lucky because we had Ethel's apartment. We lived there with many members of our extended family: Ethel and her baby boy, her mother-in-law and father-in-law, my parents, my brother Andor and I. It was a very crowded one-bedroom apartment. In fact, thousands of people lived in the ghetto, which comprised a very small area in the middle of town. We stayed in the ghetto for about three to five weeks. The word was going around that we would soon be shipped off somewhere to work.

I always hoped that my gentile neighbors, who were our good friends before all of this started to happen, would come around to the ghetto area so that I could get a letter out to Joe, my fiancé. But no one ever came. They were too afraid to even come near the ghetto. As young adults we were always loitering on the streets. We were bored, we had nothing to do, and we felt we were stagnating. We traded books with each other and spent a lot of time reading, especially when we could find a quiet place in which to sit down. Food was scarce and we no longer had our radios to listen to. There were no newspapers in the ghetto either, so we had no knowledge at all of what was going on in the world.

The only pleasant memories I have from the ghetto are of the cool summer evenings when we would sit together and reminisce, or talk about our dreams for the future.

As days and weeks passed without the promised work, some young couples, in their rush, got married, if the boy was not away in a labor camp. But most of them had no convenient place to consummate their marriage. There was no privacy. Wherever one turned there were people. The elders attempted to organize some kind of arrangement to accommodate these couples, but the situation was too obvious, bringing embarrassment, rather than relief, to all. The young couples only wanted a bond to hold them together in the face of their uncertain future. Come what may, in the event of separation, they would draw courage from their bond. When all seemed to be lost, the knowledge and feeling that they belonged to each other would give them the strength to survive.

The children were put in yards and out on the streets so that their mothers could cook and clean in the very limited space. Three or four families had to share a single stove on which to cook. People continuously quarreled over the use of stoves and sleeping spaces. It was crowded, and as people moved about, they had to maneuver over sleeping individuals lying on the floor. The young children were clearly bewildered and could not comprehend what was happening around them. They could not understand why they could not go home. From time to time we heard the cries of children as they sought to return to their homes. Within a very short time, crowding and frustration led to tempers, agitation, arguments and quarreling. The mothers, in particular, were nervous and perturbed, as they had to prepare food and care for their families despite the shortages and strained conditions. The men felt and behaved like trapped animals. Their sense of helplessness was aggravated by lack of activity and small tragedies, such as the lack of smoking tobacco. Most important of all, there was confusion and uncertainty due to the lack of news. There were no newspapers and no radios. No one knew what was happening in our town and in the world as a whole. Does the world know what has happened to us? Do they know that we are prisoners in our own hometown? Our homes had been locked up with most of our belongings, our precious gardens had been left unattended, and we were crowded on top of each other, idle and waiting, without knowing why.

# Chapter 3

# Leaving the Ghetto

One day the Nazis began shipping us out of town. They told us that we would be working in factories and that we should pack up our belongings. They gave us very little time, so we feverishly began packing up. We did not know what we should take and what we should leave behind, but I remember my father's foresight when he said, "Pack the hams." My father and mother kept kosher, and would not eat the ham; but they realized that we, the children, needed whatever nourishment we could get. So my parents had decided to take along the ham, whether it was kosher or not. We took our bedding with us as well. We were allowed to take only a certain weight, in specified kilograms, per person. Later, I wished that they would not have allowed us to take anything, because we were so terribly overcrowded in the cattle cars in which they had stuffed us. There was absolutely no room. About eighty of us were packed inside one cattle car and we had to sit on our own belongings. There was no space to lie down, no chairs or benches, nor was there enough room to stretch out in any way.

When we left town we had to walk, carrying all our belongings to the train station. Our arms were loaded down, and I remember holding a letter to my fiancé in my hand, hoping, once again that I could find someone who would mail it for me. No such person was to be found. Instead, I underwent one of the most painful experiences of disappointment and humiliation as I saw some of our townspeople, including some of our neighbors, standing by and spitting at us, yelling at us "Good, now we'll get rid of the Jews," and similar words. The more decent people simply did not come out to show their faces at all. To this day I feel hurt at the knowledge that our very own long-time neighbors had made no attempt to somehow help us or to protest what was happening. It was this experience that made me determined not to return to my home town ever again.

The conditions in the cattle car were intolerable. Obviously, there were no toilet facilities, not even the most primitive. We were compelled to relieve ourselves in front of everyone, without even minimal privacy. We used buckets, which were then passed on to the people situated near a single tiny window in the back. Someone then disposed of the contents of the bucket by emptying them through the small opening. We had no drinking water nor any water for washing up. Ethel had her two-year-old son, Gyurika, with her. He was a beautiful little boy with blond curly hair. She had brought diapers for him but we could not find them or get to them. During the train ride, he was inflicted with a terrible rash and cried continuously. Ethel's husband, Bandi, had been taken to a forced-labor camp in 1942, and she had not heard anything from him or about him since his departure.

It did not take long before it started to smell in the car. The crowding, the lack of clean air, the need to relieve ourselves, all contributed to an increasing stench and to breathing difficulties. Physically, I was the strongest of all my family members, and I struggled to get as close as I could to the tiny window at the end of the car. I wanted to hold Gyurika near the window for some fresh air. Packed into the cattle cars, we were locked inside, kept on a dead railroad track for hours. We were put on display before our home-town people, subjected, like animals in a zoo, to hours of humiliation.

It had also gotten very hot in the cattle car, as it was the beginning of summer. We left on May 21, and arrived at Auschwitz on May 24. Those three days in the cattle car were pure hell. Many old people were crying. Weakened and exposed to the unsanitary conditions, many people became physically sick. Several did not survive the journey. I could hear people shouting, "Oh! He's dead, he's dead!" We had to ride with the dead bodies alongside. Our own survival, however, preoccupied all our thoughts. We were much too involved with our own attempts to remain alive to pay too much attention to the dead amongst us.

We concentrated on keeping our family together. We shared the little food that we had with us. Some people had brought fruit and we had brought egg biscuits, which we had baked at home before entering the ghetto. Luckily, my mother had thought ahead. She said, "We are going on a train, and we don't know where they are taking us, so we must take some egg biscuits...something to eat." The biscuits were made with flour and eggs and were nourishing. Traditionally, we had kept a kosher diet at home. With his foresight, however, my father had managed to buy some non-kosher foods on the black market. He was thinking of his children, and the need for nourishment was his main concern.

What we did not have but needed desperately was water. After we had been on the train for two days, the train guards brought us a large can of water. We had to use what we could immediately and we were not able to save any for the remainder of the journey. When they took the water away, we had no more of the precious liquid to use until the next water delivery. We were given very little water and very infrequently.

Occasionally, the train made a stop for ammunition pickups or for other reasons. Those were the worst times, because we would just be parked in the heat of the day, for hours upon hours. When the train moved, there was some air movement in the crowded and sweltering car and the little lone window provided some ventilation. In addition, the motion created a perception and a feeling that we were going somewhere and that we were nearing some destination that would relieve us of our misery. With every movement of the train came renewed hope that, eventually, there would be an end to this miserable journey out of Hungary.

Just before crossing the border, the Hungarian gendarmes (the border guards, who were usually very cruel) stopped the train, approached our car and said, "We know that you dirty Jews didn't give up all your valuables. Give us whatever you have left! We know that you are stealing them and that you are trying to take them with you! Give them up now or we'll search each one of you. If we find any valuables on you, we will shoot you right here in front of the rest!" In actuality, we had given up almost everything. All we owned had been taken from us before we went into the ghetto. Andor, my brother, was a tailor and had sewn some money into his shirt cuff. My poor mother was very frightened. She kept telling Andor, "Give it up, give it up!" Andor did not know how to get the paper bills out, since he had sewn them into the garment. Somehow, someone passed us a razor blade and Andor cut the cuff and gave up the money. However, in his haste and excitement, he cut a bill in half and the other half remained in his shirt cuff. After the Gendarmes had collected everyone's valuables, one of them came up with the half bill and said, "Where is the other half of this? Who dropped this in the hat? Give it up or else you will all be shot. We have no remorse. We have no pity for you. You are all thieves." Andor suddenly realized what had happened and so did I. Immediately, I grabbed the torn bill from him, pushed him back and yelled, "It's here!" I assumed that the gendarmes would be more lenient with a young girl than they might be with a boy. The soldier told me to step down, off the car. I made my way through the bags and the people and then jumped off. He said, "Do you know what you did? You disfigured the money of our republic, and that is a crime punishable by death! We warned you!" I apologized and tried to explain, but I was too frightened and too distressed. They began to beat me as I was standing next to the cattle wagon. They beat me mercilessly, striking me with one blow after another and then threw me up against the cattle wagon. Throughout this ordeal, they were cursing and calling me names. Finally, they told me to get back onto the cattle car. My mother was clearly relieved, because she was convinced that if it had been my brother instead of me, they would have shot him dead.

As we crossed the border, we were handed over to the German soldiers and our train ride continued. We had no knowledge of our destination and we were fearful and anxious. None of this was ever known. These expulsions and transports were a well-kept secret that was never leaked out to our hometowns or to the newspapers. We had heard some things from my father, who had heard them on Voice of America radio, but we refused to believe them. Even while on this transport train, we could not comprehend, nor could we believe, that we were destined for annihilation.

We could not believe that humankind could be as cruel as our experiences to come would prove. At this stage, it was totally incomprehensible that whole families, with their children, would be taken out of their homes to carry out physical labor for the government. It was unheard of. It was totally unbelievable that we would be singled out for our religion. That could happen in the dark ages, not in 1944, we thought. After all, we reasoned and believed, there is a world community out there! My country must be responsible, if not to God then to the world.

However, fear began to creep into our hearts and we started to believe that the treatment to which we were subjected, although out of the ordinary, was now to be expected. We were not criminals, but we dared not confront cruelty and guns. We did not know how. We were defenseless, led to our fate like helpless sheep.

# CHAPTER 4

# Arrival at Auschwitz

We arrived at Auschwitz on May 24, 1944. We did not know where we were. The cattle car was opened and we saw young men in striped clothing and caps, with absolutely no hair. All of a sudden everyone was shouting. The German soldiers with their rifles and bayonets yelled, "*Aus! Aus! Mach's schnell! Mach's schnell!*" Everyone tried to grab their belongings as we jumped out in a hurry. I ran as quickly as I could to get my mother's medicine; Ethel was running frantically to secure some of her baby's belongings. The young men in the striped clothing kept saying to the young mothers, in Yiddish, "Give your child to an older person." Ethel said, "They are crazy! What do they mean give my child to an older person?" We kept trying to grab belongings, but the soldiers began beating us back. Scared by the commotion and the noise, Gyurika started to cry. My sister's mother-in-law took the boy while Ethel and I tried to get more of our belongings from the cattle car. Within a matter of a few minutes, when we turned around, we saw that her mother- and father-in-law, Gyurika, Andor and my parents had been beaten off to a line to the left of us. Ethel started to run to get Gyurika back, but a soldier hit her with the butt of his rifle and told her, "Go back, go back! Five to a row." Immediately we were forced to line up in rows of five. In the continuing chaos and turmoil we could see our family being taken away, never to be seen again. Ethel kept trying to go with them but was repeatedly beaten back by the soldiers. We watched them all go off in a different line, until we could not see them anymore.

In my mind's eye, I see my mother's desperate glance at our separation. I see her being pushed by the German S.S. guards. I see her trying to comfort her small grandson, who was crying for his mother, arms outstretched, and his mother crying, trying to break down the barricade separating them, but to no avail, as she was beaten back.

High above we saw the chimneys. With their fiery smoke, they looked so promising. They appeared to be factories, at which we would be working. A wrought-iron archway appeared to welcome us with the words *Arbeit macht frei*. This was encouraging because it translated to mean "Work makes freedom," suggesting that we would be engaged in work.

In the utter confusion of those moments we still did not comprehend what was happening to us, nor did we have a hint of what our fate was to be. Within moments we had undergone a terrible tragedy of separation, and the world did not seem to care.

Next, we found ourselves lined up in front of a handsome, elegant high-ranking officer who, we found out later, was the notorious Dr. Joseph Mengele, nicknamed the "Angel of Death." We had to walk by him while he inspected us, looking closely at our faces and bodies. Occasionally, he would ask someone their age. He would wave his hand, either to the right or to the left, ordering people into one of two directions. Ethel, I and some other people from our hometown were sent to the right and we joined a larger group. Many women were wildly hysterical over being separated from their babies. Ethel's friend, Clara, tried to fight a soldier in an attempt to go back and retrieve her baby. Meanwhile, chaos and confusion reigned throughout as the German soldiers herded us away, forcing us to walk ahead. In an effort to restore some order and to quiet the hysterical women, the soldiers kept saying, "Why are you hysterical? You are going to meet them in the baths. You are going to the bath house." Ethel and Clara just hugged each other and cried. We were forced to keep on walking while our loved ones were out of sight.

We were being marched, five in a row, silently, away from the railroads of Birkenau. This was a special railroad station, created conveniently in a location near the concentration camps and the crematoriums.

We looked around us and as far as the eye could see we were surrounded by barbed-wire fences. Within the compound we saw wooden barracks and narrow dirt roads between them. At the time, we were not aware of the fact that the wires were electrified. The silence was broken only by the gentle sobbing of young mothers mourning the loss of their babies and children.

Despite the S.S. Guards' promise that we would meet our family members at the bath house, the mothers must have sensed and felt the finality of their fate. They had emotionally experienced the inevitable: that they would not see their offspring again.

As I walked silently, I thought about my loved ones, marching within other rows of five, in different directions. How did they feel, especially since they had never been away on a holiday or a journey? Little did I know, at that moment, that my dear ones did not even have a tomorrow in their future. This march may have been their last, leading them into the bathhouses where shower heads released deadly cyanide gas instead of water.

After quite a long time, we arrived at a big red brick building. Thousands of young women, probably from earlier transport trains, were standing around. We were extremely fatigued, hungry, thirsty and exhausted, both mentally and physically. Many people sat down, but when they did, the guards yelled at them to stand up. We arrived at about four in the afternoon on a Saturday. It was the Jewish holiday of Shavuot, the day before Arbor day.

My sister Ethel and I were holding on to each other not only for support but of fear of losing each other in the ensuing chaos. We frantically held on to our handbags, which were our only possessions from home. They contained some immediate necessities such as lipstick, toothbrushes, combs and hairbrushes. But, of course, none of these belongings were to be seen or found later, after we had entered the red brick structure.

We stood around for hours and we noticed that, little by little, we were being moved. Groups of people were taken into the building. We could not see the people come out because they exited through a different door. After about six or seven hours, we entered the building. We did not know whether it was night or day, because no one had a watch. The Hungarian Gendarmes had taken them at the border crossing, along with all our other valuables, when we left our home country. We were ordered to remove all our clothing and to take only our shoes with us. As we went by, the soldiers and guards inspected us thoroughly and methodically. They looked in our shoes, in our mouths, and in our body orifices. They were looking for hidden jewels or valuables.

As we were standing there, naked, one young woman

was holding a back brace, which she had worn as an undergarment. As we passed through the door, it was grabbed by an attendant, a prisoner herself, who was selected to carry out warden duties. The brace was then thrown away onto a pile of clothes. The poor girl cried and begged, saying that she could not live without the back support, but the woman only replied, "You will," and shoved her into a room where we were to undergo disinfecting.

Only then did we begin to realize the full extent and impact of our captivity and the dehumanization inflicted with it, and that we were no longer being treated as human beings. We were being cheated, lied to, and deprived of our freedom via a systematic, step-by-step process.

We were taken into another room, where women using old dull scissors and hair clippers clipped and shaved everyone. We were completely de-haired. As we were pushed into this room we could not stay near our friends and family members, and after having been shaven we were unable to recognize each other. After finally finding our lost loved ones we embraced and broke into hysterical laughter. Slowly, the laughter turned into crying. We hugged each other and cried until we were pushed into the next room, where the showers were located.

Before we could take a shower, we were dunked into a large container, filled with a foul smelling, cold disinfecting liquid. Finally, we had our showers. It felt so good. It was one of only two occasions to shower that we had had during the entire time of our incarceration. Everyone pushed everyone else as we all tried to stay under the trickles of slightly warm water for as long as we possibly could. We had no soap, but we were so happy to get wet and a little bit clean. Suddenly all the water was turned off at once. The shower was over, and we were left without any means to dry ourselves. We were then driven out of the showers, into a huge room with long tables. On one table there were piles of clothes; on another, there were socks; a third was covered with jackets. We had almost no underwear and we still carried our own shoes with us. As we walked by the tables, we were handed pieces of clothing, at random, without regard for size, color or fit. The socks were mismatched; the dresses were either too big or too small. The stack of coats dwindled and then disappeared and many people, including myself, did not get one. We went outside and started to dress ourselves. I managed to get a black jersey dress which, luckily, was very long. This was very useful because I was able to tear pieces off the bottom to use as turbans on our heads. The weather in Auschwitz was terrible. It was very hot during the days, yet terribly cold at night. With our shaven heads we felt extremely cold.

When the whole shower ordeal was over it was about one o'clock in the morning. We were marched off to Lager C (area C). There were thirty-one wooden barracks in the Lager. These were the first lagers in Auschwitz, constructed by Polish-Jewish prisoners five years earlier. They had lived in those structures until they were murdered. When we arrived, there were at least 1,000 people in each of the barracks. Barracks 31 was empty, so we were placed there. The thirty-one barracks were set up in an oval configuration, with the center area open. The Germans used this central section to assemble us for inspections, selections, and other purposes. Each of the barracks contained a small room inside for the *Blockelteste*, who was a Polish or Slovak woman charged with the responsibility of overseeing and controlling us. They had been instructed to be very firm and tough in their treatment of the prisoners.

When we entered the barracks it was dark and the floor

was covered with mud because it had rained the previous day. In the middle of the structure there was a very long, red brick unit, resembling an oven or a heating apparatus. The first to enter the barracks ran as quickly as they could to occupy the top of this oven, hoping to benefit from the heat it promised to produce. We found out later that it was never turned on, and no heating was provided at all. By the time we entered the barrack, we had nowhere to sit but on the muddy floor. We were so tired that we could do nothing but sit down. Ethel was still crying about losing her baby.

After the showers we did not see any of our lost family members. We did not know what to think. We were extremely upset and distressed, especially Ethel. It slowly dawned on us that we were lied to when the guards said that we would meet our loved ones in the bath house. Ethel had also gotten her menstrual period, induced by the great commotion, stress and excitement. I could not let her sit in the mud, so I said to her, "It doesn't make sense for us both to get all muddy. You are smaller than I, so I'll sit in the mud, and you can sit in my lap." We were very cold, so we huddled together to warm ourselves with our body heat. We did not even know the other people who shared this space with us, but we all needed warmth, so we just joined together closely to gather warmth from each other.

At about five in the morning, it was beginning to get lighter outside and we began to recover from the overwhelming ordeal. We looked around to see what was going on and where we were. At around five-thirty the *Blockelteste* came out. She was a Slovak Jewish woman, charged with the difficult job of controlling us. She started out by warning us. "I have been here for five years," she said, "and I have seen a lot of misery. I am one of the people who built these barracks. We were in the rain, and we were in the sun. We suffered through terrible weather in this area. You, at least, have a roof over your heads. I will see to it that if you're good and if you behave yourselves, you will get food and will have a decent stay here; but if you are going to give me trouble, then I will have to give you trouble. I have to control more than a thousand people, and I am responsible for your behavior. I have to answer to the German soldiers. I am responsible for you, and Graise will come to see that I am doing my job and that you are being good. You will see Graise later. She is a beautiful blonde lady, but she is very mean and cruel. If you rock the boat in any way, you will find yourself under it. Do you see those chimneys over there? Do you see the flames and smoke that come out? Do you smell the flesh? That is where they are burning your families." It was then that we realized what was going on. But still, we could not believe that what she said was true.

Only women were placed in these barracks. The men were all taken elsewhere. All the women were between seventeen and thirty-five years of age. They had been the only ones selected by Dr. Mengele to live, because they were strong enough to work. The *Blockelteste* ordered some of the girls to go to her room and bring out sixteen sticks. She handed the sticks to the tallest, youngest and strongest looking girls. Ethel and I were among those selected. With a stern voice she went on to say, "This is your duty. You girls are to be my helpers. You are going to be *Stubediensten*" ("servants," in German). "You must help me control this group and you will use these sticks whenever necessary."

She finished and returned to her room. Ethel and I looked at each other and we knew that we could not use the sticks and be her "servants." After they let us out for what was called "free block" (when the occupants of all thirty-one barracks were allowed out to walk and mingle), we decided that since nobody knew yet who we were, we would just put down the sticks and go into another barrack. As we walked around and mingled among the crowd, we discovered some acquaintances in Block 10. They were friends of my uncle. Also in the same block, we found Rose and Lilly, the sisters of Joe, my fiancé. They had their own spaces in a bunk. We realized that we would not need to remain in the mud in our original barrack. Of course, the barrack was crowded and fully occupied. However, along with everyone else, we scrambled and pushed and beat each other off and bargained as we tried to secure some space on a bunk, each of which accommodated twelve to fourteen people crowded, side by side, head by feet in alternating order.

Slowly, people found their friends and relatives and moved from one block to another. We too had managed to settle in with people we knew. With all the place exchanges, bartering and trading, we were in business. The working system was based on barter and trade. We exchanged clothes with people who had others that fit better. We traded bread for a needle to sew with. We were constantly haggling. Once someone settled into a place, others did not take it away from them. We found my older sister, Miriam, who was about thirty-six years old, with her seventeen-year-old daughter, Irene. Irene had had a limp ever since her childhood days. She had undergone many operations to remedy her deformed knee and leg, but remained with a permanent limp. Somehow she had slipped past Dr. Mengele's notice during the inspection.

Miriam was from the town of Kolosvar, about 300 kilometers away from Satu-Mare, where we had lived. She was a very tall and beautiful woman and Irene was also very pretty. Without her hair she looked like a beautiful young boy. They were originally placed in Block 12, but after our reunion we moved them into Block 10 to be with us.

# CHAPTER 5

# Daily Life in Auschwitz

Every morning at about five, as well as every afternoon, we had to line up for "roll call." Graise, or someone else, would come and count us. She was a beautiful blonde woman, smartly dressed in an officer's uniform, with shiny black leather boots. She was usually on horseback, with her nail-studded whip in hand. Sometimes we had to stand in line for hours. If someone did not feel well and sat down, our *Blockelteste* would try to ignore it, but she would remind us, "Girls, you've got to stay standing, because if you get caught sitting, Graise will give you twenty-five lashes." We had to stand in rows of five, usually with the same people in each row. We could choose by whom to stand and the four of us, Ethel, Miriam, Irene and I, needed one more person to complete a group of five.

We chose a Slovak girl to join us. We needed to choose someone with whom we knew we would get along, because we all had to share one loaf of bread. Every evening, after the roll call, we would get a single loaf of bread, about half of which was made of sawdust mixed in with the flour. We did not care much about the bread ingredients because we were constantly and continuously hungry. We needed to divide the bread loaf equally into five pieces, without the benefit of a knife or other cutting instrument. When we had arrived in Auschwitz we were only given a spoon, a cup and a small bowl with a hole in the side, all made of dark red enamel. We would wear our eating tools on a strip of cloth, torn from our dresses, strung through the holes in the utensils and worn around our waists. If you lost your bowl, you were out of luck because new bowls were not provided. We sharpened the handles of our spoons on a rock so that we could use them as knives to cut our bread with. We tried to divide the bread evenly and equally down to the last crumb! The five of us felt that we were responsible for each other.

The Slovak girl had told us about what happened when the Slovak and Transmistrian Jews were taken away from their homes. She told of how they were tortured, raped, and humiliated; forced to eat their own feces and shot into the graves that they had been forced to dig. We did not know about all these atrocities until we were already incarcerated ourselves. Somehow the Nazis were able to keep these terrible deeds a secret until it was too late for the Jews. Even today, I often wonder how they were able to keep these atrocities bottled up so well. From the late 1930s until the 1940s, when my father began hearing the news on Voice of America, no information leaked out. We were totally ignorant of these happenings. Most of the other Jews were kept in the dark even more than we were, because they had no access to radios, newspapers or other sources of information. We only knew what little we did because we violated the rules by defiantly listening to radio broadcasts that we were not allowed to listen to. The general population was also ignorant about what was going on, because few people owned radios. Most were not even aware of the existence of the Voice of America. Besides, since the news media were censored, there was no freedom of the press at all.

I had the misfortune of tasting Graise's whip on one occasion. After the guards had locked up all the barracks, we were not permitted to be outside at all. The soldiers would usually come at that time and select women for whatever purpose they needed, and for hours upon hours we were required to stay inside. I had gone around to the kitchen to see if I could find some work to do in exchange for food, or even to steal some food for my family. I always shared whatever I could get. Those who happened to be around the kitchen when the bread truck was being unloaded were sometimes able to help out in exchange for being permitted to keep some of the broken bread pieces that had fallen onto the ground. I would tie up my dress and put the bread pieces in it. On some mornings I was there as early as four o'clock, before the roll call, so as to be able to "organize" some food. One morning I was there when the guards sounded the *Blockspaare* horn, which meant that everyone had to run quickly and get into the barracks. I was too far away from my building and I could not make it back in time. Graise saw me running, attempting to get back as quickly as I could. She dismounted her horse and chased me. She hit me with her whip, but partially missed, inflicting only minor pain, because I dashed into the nearest barrack, out through the opposite doorway, and then in and out of the other barracks, until I was safely back in my own building. She lost sight of me. I was very lucky. That was the only time I tasted her whip.

Our daily occupation was simply a continuous effort to survive. In the morning we had some "coffee." It was not real coffee, but warm water steeped with burnt bread crumbs, without any sugar or milk; but it was better than nothing. When we were allowed to stay out of the barracks, we could spend some time taking care of our basic necessities. The toilets were only holes in the ground, lined up within a long building. There was a "bath" house which had rows of low faucets where we could wash ourselves, but could not take a bath or a shower. We could wash our clothes there as well, but with water only. Soap was not provided, nor was it available. We then placed the wet clothes on our backs to dry in the sun as we moved about outside.

By afternoon, we would usually be tired and we tried to find some shaded areas in which to lie down. The sun was very hot, and it was difficult to find a shady spot. We constantly spent our time in efforts to find food. We looked for a little bit of grass or greenery to chew on; it was a scarce commodity, and when we were lucky enough to find some it tasted like a delicacy. For lunch, our *Stubediensten* would roll in a large container of food. They ladled food into our bowls as we lined up to get it; it consisted mainly of grass and cabbage with an occasional sliver of meat. When we found a piece of potato in the soup, we felt very fortunate. Sometimes the soup contained a little bit of grease. They kept us on very few calories. Only enough to barely keep us alive. We were rapidly losing weight and we looked very bad. At first we could not stand the taste of the food. The Germans put "bromo" in it to stop us from menstruating. It seemed they also added some sort of tranquilizers to keep us calm and indifferent. After a few days we were no longer concerned about what was in our food. We were so hungry that we could have eaten a stone. I did not get my period throughout the time that I was confined in the camps. Ethel had hers only once, just after she arrived.

At night we were given the single loaf of bread which was divided among the five of us. It came with a small square of margarine and every once in a while with a tiny piece of cheese, or with marmalade. That was all the food that we were given daily. Most of the time, when cheese was included in the day's portion it was not edible, as it was crawling with maggots. The French women loved it, though. They considered the maggots to be added protein and said that it kept them alive. We could not stomach it, so we often traded the cheese for bread, for thread, or something else.

In my idle days I would wrack my brain to figure out how to get more food. I suddenly had an idea when one of my socks started to unravel. I pulled the thread and made a small ball out of it. Then I traded something for a very large button that I had seen on a girl's dress. With a precious needle, obtained through more bartering and trading, I revisited my childhood memories and created a doll's head with long hair by covering the button with light-colored material I had torn off my clothes or my underwear. I created several dolls. I made their faces pretty and attractive. Each of the dolls had different color hair, depending on whose socks I managed to obtain. Of course, I only used the upper leg section of the socks, because no one in her right mind would be willing to give up the only pair of socks she owned. I created the doll's body, complete with arms and legs, by using pieces of clothes obtained by trading with other people. My major investment was a pair of manicure scissors, for which I had to pay with bread, which was the most precious commodity.

This project was a blessing for me during the four and a half months I spent in Auschwitz. It provided an occupation and a way to obtain food. As soon as I finished a doll, we would trade it to the *Blockeltesten* for food. They, in turn, gave my dolls as gifts to the German officers, with whom we were not able to have direct contact. To the Germans, we were non-entities, and we were not permitted even to approach them. For them we were nothing but numbers.

Upon our arrival at Auschwitz we had been stripped of all our possessions and belongings, except for our shoes. Some items and possessions, however, found their way into the camp in what seemed to be mysterious ways. Actually, precious items such as needles and scissors were obtained through a complicated process. For example, next to Lager C, in which I was held, was another concentration area, Lager A. It was separated from us by an electrical wire fence. Shortly after our arrival, Joe's sisters Rose and Lilly had been moved from Lager C to Lager A, which was next to the men's Lager. Several women, including Rose and Lilly, had friends on the men's side. These men worked at the railroad and labored at emptying the wagons as more transports of Jews arrived at Birkenau, Auschwitz. They were the men we had seen upon our arrival. As they cleaned out the wagons, they were able to take and conceal some of the abandoned items that the newly arrived Jews had left behind. Then they smuggled these items into their camp. Sometimes, out of generosity, they threw some of these items over or through the electric fence to Rose and Lilly, who waited on the other side. One day, one of Lilly's friends who was still in Lager C approached me with a whole head of garlic which Lilly had asked her to give me. This was a very precious commodity, because I could sell it—one clove at a time—to the kitchen cooks. The kitchen workers had food, but no seasonings. I traded the garlic for food. One time, Lilly's friend instructed me to meet Lilly and Rose at the fence after the roll call. When I met them, they threw a large block of a substance over the fence. It looked like solidified honey. It was wonderful! It was huge! It measured about one foot in length by approximately six inches in width and it was two inches deep. We ate this sweet matter and traded some of it for many useful things and for other foods. We made arrangements to meet again on the following day, at the same time. That was the last time I saw them in Auschwitz. On the next day, and on the following days, I looked for them frequently but without success. Only after our liberation I learned that Lilly and Rose had been transferred to a work camp. There they labored at an ammunition factory until the end of the war and were lucky to live under more tolerable conditions.

One day a musical band arrived at Auschwitz. We could not take our eyes off the girls. They wore such beautiful clothes! And they had such nice long hair! We assumed that they were Germans, but later we found out that they were Jews, selected because of their musical talents and their ability to entertain. We felt so inferior to them. They were so beautiful and we looked like animals! We never found out the purpose of their visit or the reason for their entertainment stop in the camp.

Every once in a while the German soldiers came by to look for people with one talent or another. Sometimes they looked for girls with "beautiful eyes." We were fearful that they might attempt to use us as prostitutes for the soldiers in the war front because we had heard rumors that some girls were taken away for that purpose. At one time, when we had volunteered to deliver blankets from a neighboring camp, we met several French and Belgian girls who had been used as prostitutes. So we knew that the rumors were well-founded. Apparently, and luckily, we were not designated for such duties. We probably looked much too terrible. We must have appeared far from attractive with our malnourished bodies and shaven heads.

Some people in the camp were too weak, both mentally and physically, to survive. Some became apathetic or psychotic. These people lost all hope and held no will to continue their daily struggle to remain alive. We had to deal with these people continuously; to talk to them, try to provide some encouragement or comfort, and sometimes forcefully hold them down to keep them from running to the electric wire fences in a desperate attempt to end their misery. One needed only to touch the fence with a single finger to be electrocuted and die. People regularly committed suicide on the fence and their bodies were often found on the wires.

On some days we were subjected to an examination and selection process, the purpose of which was not known to us. We were always fearful of these actions because we were concerned that Irene, my niece, inflicted with a deformed leg, would be discovered, selected and killed. This worry led us to constantly devise and attempt ways of finding out at which barracks the selection was carried out. When we discovered that the next scheduled selection was to take place in our quarters, we managed to sneak out into a different barracks to avoid discovery. We were successful a number of times, but at other times we were not able to get away. In our attempts to protect my niece, we devised a plan that we put into motion every time we were forced to go through the selection process. Typically, everyone outside the barracks was required to undress completely for inspection and selection. Completely naked, with our clothes hung over one arm, we were lined up and required to walk past a line of medical doctors who carried out the selection. Our plan involved my sister Ethel, who would go first, followed by Irene, whose clothes hung over her arm in a way which partially concealed her deformed leg. I would follow very closely behind her, and as she approached the doctors, I would create a distraction by tripping, pushing into her and shoving her quickly past the doctors. This diversion focused attention on me, allowing Irene to create the impression that her limp was caused by my fall. Her mother, Miriam, would follow behind me, because she was always terribly frightened of the possibility of losing her daughter. We were very concerned that Miriam would not be able to initiate the diversion if she were to be the one to stumble. I felt that I should take the risk myself, rather than leaving it to Ethel, because I felt an extreme sense of sorrow and pity for her. We assumed that her husband, Bandi, was dead, since we had heard nothing about him or from him since he was taken away to the forced-labor camp. (We found out much later that he had been in a Russian prison for two years prior to our incarceration. Bandi was released from the Russian prison camp in August 1948. He had spent six years in prison.) We had also despaired for Ethel, losing her beautiful son in the gas chambers upon our arrival. This terrible experience had weakened her terribly, both spiritually and physically. I felt that, compared to the others, I had been through the least amount of emotional and physical tribulation. I was unattached, more resourceful, inventive, and bolder at taking chances. Physically, I was the strongest of the four of us, determined in the thought that whatever consequences we would have to endure, it would be best if I should be the one, rather than my family, to take the punishment.

Our plan to protect Irene was successful twelve times. On the thirteenth attempt our luck ran out. Miriam and Irene were selected and placed off to one side. We did not want to proceed without them, so as we were pushing and shoving through the crowd of women undergoing the inspection, Ethel and I managed to make our way toward Miriam and Irene and join them, regardless of the guards' directions. We ignored the doctors, and stubbornly followed my sister and her daughter. It seems that no one had noticed, nor appeared to care. In the process, we lost sight of the Slovak girl who was the fifth member of our group. We were never able to find out what her fate was. In this new grouping we once again had to organize ourselves into lines of five. Another woman joined us and we were marched off to the bathhouse to be cleaned up.

At the bathhouse, we once again went through the chaos and confusion of our first encounter with the facility, which we had experienced upon our arrival in Auschwitz. We had not the slightest notion of what was going to happen to us. We did not know if we were going to be sent to work, to another camp location or, worst of all, to the crematoriums. By this time, we had become aware of the gas chambers and their continuous functioning. We saw them being operated all day and all night, without ever stopping. In the chaos of the bathhouse we suddenly noticed that Irene had disappeared. She was nowhere to be found. Miriam became frantic and hysterical. We began searching the crowd for her. At the same time, we tried desperately to delay our entrance to the bathhouse, as we needed more time to search for Irene. We did not dare to lose sight of each other, fearing that we would lose each other in the tumultuous surroundings. Finally, after what seemed like an eternity, we regained some measure of orientation and, filled with grief over the loss of my niece, we were forced into the bathhouse. It was extremely cold and all the while, while searching for Irene, we were naked and close to freezing. We made our way into the bathhouse structure and suddenly there was Irene! She was sitting by the door waiting for us! A woman prisoner who worked at the bathhouse had noticed the pretty girl with the deformed leg as she was standing naked with the others. This woman knew that Irene was in serious danger of being eliminated if a German officer happened to notice her deformity. She quickly and forcefully grabbed Irene and pushed her into the building, through a side door. She placed her index finger on her lips to suggest to Irene to be quiet. The woman was a Polish Jew who shared no common language with Irene. They communicated through gestures and Irene indicated to her that her family was still outside. The Polish woman signaled her to keep quiet and to sit tight because her family would eventually be coming in. So Irene just sat and waited until we entered. We were so glad to see her!

CHAPTER 6

# Working in Purskau

After the selection process and the quick showers, we were taken to the railroad station. Contrary to our fears, we were ordered onto a regular train, rather than the cattle-drawn wagons we had expected. It was October, and we dared hope that we were being taken to freedom, since, for the first time in a long while, we were treated as humans. While still compelled to use our old shoes, we were given coats. Those unfortunates without shoes had to continue to do without, coping with the approaching winter weather. The only shoes available to us were Dutch wooden clogs, which rubbed our feet and caused deadly blisters and infections.

The train looked beautiful and we were elated to be getting out of Auschwitz. We were upbeat and cheerful and we sang songs as the day progressed. We were certain that our luck had turned and that our lives would become better soon. On the train we could no longer smell the odor of burning flesh emanating from the gas chambers' chimneys. Nor did we have to see the fire and smoke of the crematoriums and be constantly reminded of our lost loved ones. We spent much time reminiscing and falling back on memories of the past. We did not know what the future held for us, so we talked about our past instead.

Of course, we were not freed. The train ride lasted for about a day and a night, or perhaps two days and a night. It is difficult to remember. We were taken to Silesia and disembarked. From there we were marched to Purskau, a nearby village. Our transport consisted of about 2,000 women. At nightfall we were led into two large silos, where the bedding consisted of nice deep straw. There was a very large, round drum heater in the middle of the silo. It was early winter and the weather was getting cold. We were given some food and left in the silos for the night.

Early the next morning, at about five o'clock, we were awakened for roll call. We were then marched over a three-mile stretch into a field. On our way, as we walked, we were able to pick some food, including brussels sprouts that local farmers had left behind. Every once in a while, we managed to jump out of the marching line of people to grab whatever food we could spot. We did not find much, but the little we were able to salvage at least provided something to chew on. While most of what we found was frozen, it was nutritious. We ate the stalks and what little sprouts we found on them. At first I did not even know what it was that I was eating. We did not have brussels sprouts in my country, and I only knew that it was something green and nutritious.

As we arrived at our destination we noticed several waiting groups of men wearing civilian clothing. We found out that they were the engineers whose task it was to teach us what to do. We were given shovels and other tools and were told to start digging ditches, which the men referred to as *Pancelgraben*. Each ditch was to be dug in the shape of a trapezoid, measuring four meters at the top and one half meter at the bottom. The ditches were to become traps and obstacles designed to slow down and halt advancing American and Russian tanks.

Our daily routine in Purskau consisted of getting our morning coffee and then going to work. At noon, some food was delivered to us in a cattle wagon, but much of it spilled out on the way, before ever reaching us. By the time the food arrived, not much was left. We received our cup of food, ate it, and immediately returned to work.

As we worked, we continuously tried to get closer to our friends and family members. Frequently, we made new acquaintances and friends as we worked with other women. One woman we befriended was the daughter of a very rich man from Kolosvar, my sister Miriam's hometown. Miriam was very familiar with the store that the woman's family had owned, which was very big, specializing in materials for the making of suits. Her name was Eva Molnar. Her parents were very wealthy and their children had enjoyed a privileged and comfortable childhood. The woman we met had been sent to various places in Europe to gain her schooling and education. She told stories about life in such far away places as Paris and London. She had a wealth of experience beyond what we could perceive as possible. We also befriended a French girl who seemed totally out of place with us. When she told us her own horror story, we understood how she ended up with us. My own experience had never taken me farther than to my sister's homes, which were located about 300 kilometers away. At one time I had the occasion to visit the capital of Hungary, Budapest. That was the extent of my experiential familiarity with the world. At the labor camp, we enjoyed hearing about these women's memories and experiences. Their stories sounded as remote, esoteric and foreign to us as did a journey to the moon. We all became good friends. Time appeared to pass much faster and their stories took our minds off the hard work, the harsh weather, and our constant hunger. The worst part of our conversations involved discussions of food and exchanges of recipes. They painfully reminded us of how hungry we were. But we managed to take our minds off these concerns as we talked about many other things, including the theater, music, and almost everything else.

With the arrival of winter, the work became increasingly difficult. Our shovels and picks were not very effective as we pounded the frozen earth. The engineers had resorted to dynamiting the ground, after which we were directed to move in with our shovels to remove the debris and shattered pieces of frozen earth. We had to constantly keep a watchful eye on everyone, especially on the younger and older women. Many of them had reached a point of lost hope and disillusionment about the future. They simply stopped working, sat down on the ground, and quickly froze to death. If we turned our backs as someone sat down it would sometimes be too late. By the time we took notice of someone who had given up, and before we had an opportunity to rouse the woman and encourage her to go on, it would be too late. It was so freezing cold that the mere touch of someone's frozen fingers would cause them to break off. We had to keep fully attentive and vigilant. We continuously attempted to provide encouragement and strengthen spirits by lecturing and reminding each other that there would be a brighter future, and that one day this terrible reality would end! The winter in Purskau was a long and torturous one. Technically, it extended from October until January 21, 1945. But mentally and psychologically it lasted for ages. We lost many girls who succumbed to exhaustion and the frost.

My sisters and I were very lucky to have befriended one of the foremen. He was an older person, fifty to fifty-five years of age. He noticed that I was a conscientious worker and that Ethel and I understood the nature of our work. We were able to make the sides of the *Pancelgraben* nice and straight, as he wanted. Every day he left some of his own food in the bottom of his dish and gave it to us. Sometimes he gave the leftovers to Ethel and sometimes to me. On other occasions he offered the food to someone else. Consequently, about two or three times each week we were fortunate to have some real food, without bromo in it.

We had a major problem with my niece, Irene. Because of her bad leg we had to drag her along with us out to work every day. It had become very difficult for her to walk and to keep up with the rest of us and with the work. With each passing day we had to walk farther and farther than before. The effort had become extremely demanding for Irene and, consequently, for us as well. She kept saying that she was going to do something about this situation. She planned to talk to the German guard about it. We were very frightened of the possible results of these intentions. We were afraid that if the Germans were to discover that she was crippled, they would take her away—perhaps back to Auschwitz—or, worse yet, kill her. We tried to persuade her to abandon her plans, and we offered to carry her back and forth between our camp to the work areas.

The German *Wehrmacht* was a man of about fifty years, and he lived in a small prefabricated house just outside the silos in which we were locked up for the night. Two women prisoners had been sent from Auschwitz to be in charge of us. One was named Julcsa. She was the *Lagerelteste*, the head attendant under the Germans, in charge of about 2,000 prisoners. She was the only non-Jewish person among us, as far as we knew. She had married a Jewish man and they had two sons. She had come along with them when they were incarcerated because she had thought that, being non-Jewish, her family would be spared. They were not. This experience transformed her into an extremely bitter person. Like us, she was torn away from her family and did not know whether or not they were dead or alive. She was a captive and a prisoner, just like the rest of us. She directed her bitter emotions, words and behavior at us. She was very cruel. When we had arrived, she gave us a long lecture and said, "You will all die! I will be the only one to be left alive because I am not Jewish. If you get out of line, I will have you sent back to Auschwitz where you will burn like your mothers, fathers and children." She was of Slovak origin, and we had perceived most Slovaks as rather negative in their treatment and relationships with Jews. She spoke Hungarian with a distinct Slavic accent, which clearly distinguished her from the others. Under her command was Marcsa, her helper, the *Blockelteste*, a Czech woman who had with her a very beautiful seventeen-year-old niece. Through this "connection" the Czech enjoyed the privilege of not having to work in the fields with us. Instead, she was given the job working for the old *Wehrmacht* man. She became his housekeeper and cooked for him. As a result, she was able to spend her nights inside his warm dwellings and to have ample food. My niece who, like the rest of us, was aware of this arrangement said one day, "If she can do it, so can I." Obviously, the Czech woman's position was well protected by her Slovak patron, and Irene could not perceive of a way to find a similarly convenient work arrangement. But she was determined to get an indoor job somehow, somewhere. We were constantly worried about Irene and we continuously tried, as hard as we could, to dissuade her from exposing her bad leg to this man.

One morning, to our horror, Irene jumped out of the line during roll call, ran up to the *Wehrmacht*, lifted up her pant leg and showed him her atrophied leg. In the broken German that she spoke, she quickly explained that it was very difficult for her to walk to the work area every day and that she could work hard in the kitchen and keep the place clean. She promised that she would work diligently and that she would become his best worker. When he saw her leg, the *Wehrmacht* appeared stunned. He was amazed that she had managed to survive as long as she had, despite the on-going process of culling out of the old, the sick and the injured people back in Auschwitz. How did she get through the selection process without ever being discovered and sent to the gas chamber? He seemed to be truly impressed by her ability to survive. He immediately told Julsca to find Irene a job and to let her work within the compound.

This incident infuriated the Slovak woman. She was clearly angry, and after the *Wehrmacht's* departure, she summoned Irene and attacked her physically, beating and hitting her wildly. "How dare you disgrace me by going over my head, straight to the commandant!" she said. "I am the boss here, and if you have a problem come straight to me! If any of you does something like this again I'll send you back to Auschwitz, or I'll kill you right here myself!" Her rage and actions had terrorized us immensely, to the point that, since that day, no one dared to do something like that again.

My niece survived the beating and went to work within the living compound. It became her responsibility to keep the premises clean, both inside and around the silos. Since she happened to be around the kitchen at times, she was able to steal some food for us. Every once in a while, as we returned to the living quarters at the end of the day, we found small portions of food hidden away underneath the straw heaps on which we slept. Sometimes Irene was the one to dish out the food into our bowls. She saw to it that the older mothers and those mostly in need would get a few more potatoes or other additions to their meager portions. She could not favor us, of course, and her sense of fairness and kindness compelled her to care for those in need. Sometimes she was able to gather some potato peels which she handed out as well. It was food too, and we consumed anything that we could secure. We would dry these peels by the heater and eat them. The peels came from the guards' food, not ours.

The only bedding material we possessed was a blanket, given to each of us when we had arrived at Purskau. We used the blanket for cover at work, to protect us from the bitter cold and to keep away the rain and snow. In the silos, along with the straw, the blanket served as our bed. The weather had turned so cold as the winter took hold that while working in the field we had to find ways of keeping warm. We stuffed straw inside our coats for warmth. We looked like human scarecrows. After a while, we were no longer allowed to stuff our clothing and we had to leave the straw behind, in the silos.

One day, after arriving at our compound, back from work, we were all lined up and blood portions were extracted from each of us. There was no explanation given for the blood collection and we assumed that the blood was to be shipped to the front lines, for soldiers who had been injured. Each blood portion was identified by the giver's name, which puzzled us, because in prior blood extractions we were never asked for our names. As far as the German authorities were concerned, we were all nameless Jews whose identities were not a matter of significance or importance. A few days later, several people's names were announced. That was when we discovered that the blood extractions had been used to test us for typhus. Those whose test results were positive were taken away and placed within two prefabricated sheds. Miriam was one of the women diagnosed as afflicted. She was placed in one of the sheds, along with four others. Each shed contained two bunk beds with straw. The sheds were kept locked and there was only one small window through which we could communicate with the women inside. Irene was able to steal more straw for the captives and passed it to them through the window, along with some food. Whenever she managed to secure some additional food without getting caught, she smuggled it through to her mother and the others inside the shed. The inflicted women did not appear to be sick. However, under the circumstances, considering all that we had gone through, none of us looked healthy anyway. As time went by, the locked-up women became increasingly weak, and their condition was exacerbated by lack of fresh air and the inability to move about or get physical exercise.

There was a makeshift hospital within the compound. It was called a hospital but it hardly resembled a real one. It was ill-equipped and contained virtually nothing with which to treat people. It was most frequently used to treat frostbite that had occurred during work. A typical frostbite treatment consisted of placing greasy margarine-wrappers onto frozen fingers or toes. Some of those diagnosed with typhus, especially the women who had become very weak, were also "hospitalized."

# CHAPTER 7

# The Death March

On the twenty-first of January 1945 we returned to the silos after a day's work and were told to gather all our belongings because we were moving out. We were very worried about Miriam, who was locked up in the shed. We were being rushed and everyone was scrambling to get their belongings and to get out. We were told to get into our lines of five again. While these activities were happening and as a state of total chaos ensued, we noticed that Miriam, along with other typhus-infected women, was moved into the "hospital." We were deliberately slow in getting into our line and stalled as much as we could. In the midst of the commotion and the great confusion we succeeded in fetching Miriam—actually kidnapping her—out of the hospital. She quickly lined up with us in our row.

The orders to leave were apparently as much of a surprise to our guards as they were to us. It was about midnight before we were finally organized to move. Each group of five women was given a single loaf of bread to share but, for a change, it was *real* bread, same as the bread given to the Germans, rather than our usual sawdust brand. It is probable that in their haste, our guards did not have enough time to prepare our usual bread, as the orders to evacuate came as a complete surprise. Before the start of the march out, all the "hospitalized" people, about forty in all, were loaded onto wheelbarrows. Most of them were in desperate shape, clearly beyond help and hope. Many of them were delirious and had no understanding of what was happening. The Germans must not have had the orders to shoot them, or I think they would have. Then the guards came around and selected those who looked most fit and ordered us to push the wheelbarrows as we started moving. I was chosen for the task with several others I knew.

We began to march through the snow, which had frozen and turned into shiny ice. It was very difficult to walk. Our shoes were the same old worn-out street shoes with which we had arrived in Auschwitz—some even had heels. We could barely stand on the ice. We slipped and fell continuously. We had to hold onto each other for support. I was somewhat luckier then some of the others for I had taken good care of my shoes, which were not in too bad a shape. On warm days at Auschwitz, I chose to go barefoot in order to save wear and tear on my shoes. I frequently walked around with my shoes slung over my shoulder and the laces tied together. At night we would sleep with our shoes under our heads for pillows. Everyone guarded their shoes carefully because those unfortunates who did not own a pair of shoes would rarely pass up an opportunity to steal someone else's. Footwear had become a precious and well-guarded piece of personal property.

As the march out began, I was stuck with the task of pushing a wheelbarrow loaded with a sick person. I was barely able to carry out this duty. The wheelbarrow constantly slipped and frequently became stuck in the slippery ice. It would not have been as bad had it been a sled, but a wheelbarrow on ice is almost impossible to push. Within a short time I had fallen behind the rest of the marching people. I became terrified by the idea that pushing the wheelbarrow would literally become my death sentence. The woman in the wheelbarrow was very sick. It was very unlikely that she would survive. I tried to talk to her but she was too weak to answer. She was completely delirious. Finally, in an act of self-preservation I abandoned her and joined the line of marchers. Other wheelbarrow pushers did the same thing. The German guards would then choose another person to push the abandoned wheelbarrows, so that an ongoing rotation system went on throughout the night.

When daylight broke the Germans needed to rest and we were stopped. It was January and extremely cold. To keep warm, we kept moving and exercising. Several women were ordered to pick up the wheelbarrows again and push them on. We saw them push their human loads away, until they had disappeared out of our sight. Then we heard shots. They shot them all dead. Then the wheelbarrow carriers returned.

One day in early February, the march was suddenly halted shortly after having paused for rest. We did not know why they stopped us, but we saw that everyone was looking off in one particular direction. We saw our *Blockelteste* rushing toward a German guard and getting his knife. Off to the side stood one of the women prisoners, with her legs spread apart. Blood was dripping onto the snow beneath her. We watched in awe as the woman gave birth to a baby out in the field, standing up all the time. The Slovak woman cut off the umbilical cord with the knife. The mother then proceeded to kill her own baby by trampling it in the snow and smashing it under her shoes. She had no other choice but to end the baby's life because it had no chance of survival. She had no milk in her breasts, nor any cloth or material in which to wrap it up. She would never have been allowed to bring a newborn along anyway. We never found out whether it had been her choice to kill the baby, or whether she had been ordered to do it. After this, we were allowed to sit and rest for about twenty more minutes and then we continued on with the march. The mother who had just lost her child continued to march with us as well. She must have become pregnant shortly before having been taken to Auschwitz and, since her pregnancy was not evident as she had undergone Dr. Mengele's inspections and selections, she managed to conceal it.

We marched on. Occasionally, when our guards could find no farm sheds or silos in which to keep us at night, we slept outside. The Nazis always had their tents, which they pitched for the night, for their own comfort and shelter. We were forced to sleep under the open skies, even if it was raining or snowing. Often we awoke the next morning to find that someone who had fallen asleep next to us had died during the night. Whenever this happened, the person nearest to the deceased individual "inherited" the dead woman's meager possessions. Under the circumstances, we did not consider such acts to be stealing. After all, the person was dead and could no longer use those few belongings any more. To actually steal from another individual was a taboo, almost unheard of except in the case of shoes. There was a sense of camaraderie and partnership. We felt that we were all in the same predicament together. We tried to help each other whenever we could. For example, if someone was too weak to march and was at the end of the line, some of the stronger women would typically go back, from the front of the marching group, to provide physical help and encouragement, for those who lagged too far behind were shot and left behind.

The people who died along the way were simply left there, where they fell. We could not take the time nor did we have the energy to bury them. The Nazis certainly did not care to spend time or effort to bury the dead. Back in Purskau, however, we did bury those who died of cold. We were with the *Wehrmacht* then and they allowed people from our group to bury the dead.

We continued to march. We walked about fifteen to eighteen kilometers each day. When we had to sleep in open fields, the few guards who had to stay awake and keep their eyes on us always ordered us to remain completely flat and to not even raise our heads, or we would be shot. As we marched, the Germans tried to keep us away from towns, villages and inhabited areas. Sometimes, however, they had no choice but to march us through a town. Usually, on such occasions, the townspeople appeared stunned to see us. We must have been quite a dreadful and depressing sight. We did not know where we were. We were uncertain whether we were marching through Germany or Poland. We tried to read road signs whenever we could in an attempt to decipher the local language, but our survival was more important and our physical location was a minor concern. Later we found out the reason for the hasty evacuation: the Russians were gaining ground and were coming close to occupying the area in which we had been held.

When herded into the silos for the night, the first thing we would do was scrounge around looking for whatever edible or usable items we could find. Sometimes, we were lucky to find broken pieces of salt, which we would pocket and save as a needed substance for our survival. At other times we found some grains or cereals. Wheat was considered to be the best commodity because it was edible instantly. When wheat was found we usually consumed it immediately because we were so hungry. We stashed whatever leftovers we managed to save into our pockets or inside our shirts, whenever we could. Later we used them for trading with others for salt, a needle and thread, or bread. The latter was an especially precious and sought-after item which very few traded. Originally, when we set out on this march, there were about two thousand of us. As the long and seemingly endless journey continued, we lost close to three hundred people. They died of disease and hunger, froze, or were shot to death. At nightfall, we were divided up between the silos and were always able to find items to trade among the people, as we were joined by different women every time.

Early in the march, which has been historically named the Death March, we had met up with two friends from Satu-Mare, our hometown. They were Elza and Sari, the two sisters of Joe's best friend. Elza was inflicted with a serious problem affecting her head, which grew more and more swollen every day, until it reached the size of a watermelon. We knew that it was only a matter of time before the Germans would notice her condition and shoot her to death. We were also convinced that, lacking any possibility of treatment, she would die anyway. So one day she ducked behind a bush, attempting to hide and then escape. Sari said it was the best thing to do because, one way or another, she would die anyhow, and it was better to die in freedom than to get shot. We continued without Elza.

As we marched, we were accompanied by a wagon that the German soldiers used to cart their tents, equipment and civilian clothing, which they carried in anticipation of the approaching end of the war. They did not wish to become captured and recognized as Nazi soldiers. As we approached the towns and villages of the countryside, the Germans allowed some of the weak and those who had exhausted their strength to climb onto this wagon. This was not an act of mercy, but rather an attempt to avoid looking bad as we walked through inhabited areas. However, one day we began to notice that sometimes the wagon would disappear after having gone through a town. Then we heard gunshots and the realization came: they shot the people on the wagon!

One day I saw Sari climb onto the Germans' wagon. I shouted to her, "Sari, don't get on the wagon! It's already afternoon and it won't be much longer. Come back! We'll help you walk!" But she would not listen to me. She said, "Without Elza, I don't want to go on anymore. I can't go on. I give up." So she and another girl from Satu-Mare boarded the wagon together.

## CHAPTER 8

# The Unknown Camp

In March of that year, we arrived at what appeared to be a camp. I did not know then, and I still do not know today, what it was called or where it was. Our group had diminished by about 500 people by that time. Our hair had grown out a bit since it was first cut in Auschwitz. It grew to the average length of a man's haircut. At this new encampment, however, our heads were shaved bald again and we were told to take off all our clothing. We then had to dunk the clothes into barrels of a disinfectant liquid, and walk ahead. Further down the line there were girls who poured more of the same smelly, cold, disinfectant over our naked bodies. We were never even given an opportunity to wash up or to take a quick shower. We had to quickly wring out our clothes and put them back on, as wet and smelly as they were.

We were then told to line up for roll call in our usual five-per-row formation. It was very cold and we were all wet and shivering. I do not know exactly what happened, but my sister Ethel was not with us in line. She had gotten into some sort of conflict with the woman who was in control of us at our barracks and the German officer took notice. The woman in charge had sent everyone to their newly assigned barracks, but told Ethel that, as punishment, she was to remain outside, in the freezing cold, throughout the afternoon. I felt sorry for my sister and, since she seemed to be the weaker of the two of us, I quickly exchanged places with her. She entered the barracks with the rest of the women and I stayed outside. I always felt a need to protect her. I remained outside throughout that afternoon, and although I suffered from the cold, I did not become sick. When I was finally allowed to go inside, I discovered three girls who had been on the same wagon with Sari and the other girl from Satu-Mare. They had been brought to this camp as well but, except for these three, had all died of starvation.

Now we had to survive in yet another camp. But this camp was absolutely bare. In the past, we had always searched for edible things as soon as we arrived in a new place. We had learned to eat just about anything that grew off the ground and anything that was green. We even ate dandelions, which were bitter and often caused stomach aches and pain. We had learned what we could eat from the Polish women in Auschwitz. We saw them washing dandelions under the faucets and they said that they contained many vitamins that would keep us alive. But in this new camp there was nothing to eat, not even a blade of grass.

There was nothing for us to do in this camp. We could walk for physical exercise, but the place appeared to offer nothing but a slow death by starvation, because we had no way to supplement the meager rations we were given. While marching, on our way here, we could eat grass and other edibles that we managed to find. Now we had become weaker and weaker and could do nothing but pray to be taken out of this camp soon.

## CHAPTER 9

# Back on the March

Finally after six weeks, we were marched out. We were glad to go, but we had lost many people due to weakness and lack of nourishment. All of us had lost our muscle tone as a result of idleness. People's legs simply gave out on them. At the time I was twenty-four years old and before my incarceration I had had a perfectly developed body. After six weeks in this camp, I had completely lost my breasts and all body fat. I remember that I was so thin that I experienced one of the worst and strangest sensations of cold air moving between my buttocks as I laid down on my side. I had the body of a boy, and at five feet, eight inches, I only weighed about eighty or ninety pounds.

We found that we were able to walk better if we could wake up early, before the German soldiers did. They slept in tents, while we had to spend the night outside, exposed to the elements. By getting up earlier, we had an opportunity to do some physical exercises just before marching. The physical activity enabled us to activate our legs and feet after sleeping outside in the snow. Often, following the cold nights we could barely walk at all in the morning. Frequently, we awoke in the morning to find dead people around us. They were just left behind.

Throughout these experiences, we became somewhat animal-like, or at least we felt less than totally human. This animal-like state of being did not take a violent form and was not manifest in incidents of physically harming each other. On the contrary, we always expressed and displayed good will and positive approaches toward each other, very often shown by helping one another. Somehow, however, we became very different than the people we used to be in our "normal," previous lifestyles. Everyone had a strong desire and will to survive. To accomplish this need, everyone was compelled to look out for herself. Nevertheless, as hard as I try, I cannot remember even a single incident in which we harmed another person. Furthermore, I cannot think of instances in which someone stole a piece of bread from a person who tried to save it. For instance, I vividly remember that as we slept outdoors, a person who was about to go to sleep said, "Oh, I must save just a bite of bread for myself to help me get up in the morning." That person, typically, would sleep through the night and no one would think of stealing her bite of bread.

Throughout the whole ordeal of Auschwitz, the forced labor, and the Death March we often wondered about the whereabouts of our loved ones. We thought about who might still be alive, and how they might be living. We found it extremely difficult to perceive of the possibility that, somewhere, people actually lived in normal houses, with regular families and children; that they actually slept with real blankets and sheets at night, in real beds. We found it difficult to even imagine what it must be like not to be constantly hungry. It is fascinating how human nature works, adapting to the realities of even the most difficult of mental and physical states. Throughout the process we suppressed memories of our earlier life to the point of finding it hard to recall. We lost weight very rapidly. We consisted mostly of just skin-covered bones. But we learned to go to sleep at night without feeling the hunger. We then woke up in the morning and did not even feel hungry! It was amazing. I still cannot understand how our human bodies cooperated with our mental state to protect us from the suffering of hunger, even though we were constantly starving. The one thing from which we were not protected, though, was our dreams. As we slept, all of us had terrible and recurring dreams about the atrocities we had experienced.

As we marched on daily, many people became exhausted and too weak to go on. Occasionally, the soldiers tried to keep us alive by giving us potatoes that they had obtained from peasants along the way, but they were under orders to shoot those who could no longer keep on marching. About six or seven of us decided to organize ourselves into a group that would help those lagging behind and having difficulties trying to keep up. Among those we helped was, of course, my niece Irene who, by the end of the day, because of her deformed leg, experienced tremendous difficulties. We had to literally drag and carry her along, as well as other women, in our attempts to keep them out of harm's way. After a few weeks of continuous daily struggle and effort, we all became terribly exhausted. We tried many different ways of carrying Irene; piggyback style on some occasions, while at other times two of us, using our arms and hands, formed a seat on which she sat as we carried her along. We resorted to whatever we could devise. Usually, we started out on the march somewhere near the front of the line, but then we gradually fell behind until we lagged dangerously far behind the marching group. All we could do at such times was hope and pray that the Germans would call for a rest stop, which would enable us to catch up with the marchers and move up again to the front of the crowd. The Germans kept insisting, "You'll be the next to be shot if you don't keep up." That frightened us so much! We were terrified that we would lose my niece. Finally, after a few weeks of marching and continuous fear we realized that if we did not do something we would eventually lose Irene. So rather then seeing her get shot to death, we devised a plan to help her and her mother, Miriam, escape. We waited anxiously for the right moment.

In the meantime we were busily engaged in our ongoing attempts to survive and to find food. As we approached inhabited areas, the German soldiers were unable to maintain full control over the large group of marchers because we knew full well that they would not shoot us inside populated villages. So when within the perimeter of a village, we took advantage of this knowledge and proceeded to run out of the line, to grab food any time we spotted something edible which appeared accessible. By that time of the year, during March and April, the sun was beginning to melt the snow. As we marched in the fields outside the villages, we spotted mounds and bulges under the thawing snow. We jumped out of line and quickly dug at these mounds, hoping to find some edible vegetation. Often we found beets or potatoes, which we stuffed inside our shirts, or wherever we could hide the precious foods. I lost a good friend, Yoli, during one of these attempts. She was shot as she ran toward a promising mound, hoping to quell her hunger.

Many times during the march we heard the sound of gunshots aimed at us. At one time, the horse-drawn wagon leading the march in front of the line was hit by a bomb. Horses were killed, and one girl's arm was blown off. In her attempt to survive, the poor girl continued to march with us, despite her terrible injuries. She kept trying to pull her clothes over the raw and bloody stump, in order to conceal her condition, but to no avail. There was very little she could do. There was nothing sterile to apply to her wounds, nor bandages or anything else to relieve her suffering. She must have suffered terribly. I do not know what became of her because we were all too busy with our own survival. Chances are that she did not march much farther with the group.

On the following morning, several girls came to the back of the marchers' line and tried to sell us pieces of meat. They were willing to trade the food in exchange for anything that we had to offer which they found to be useful, such as needles and thread, scissors, salt or grains. I do not remember what items we gave one of the girls, but we did trade some items for a few ounces of meat. We ate the meat as it was given to us, raw, because there was no possible way to cook it. We realized that even uncooked, the meat offered nourishment, no matter where it had come from. Later that day I became very ill. I was so sick that I could not continue on the march. It was late afternoon and I begged my sister Ethel to leave me behind, near the Elbe River, and to continue with the group to save her own life. I remember saying, "I can't walk another inch. Just leave me here. I'll be okay. Just go on and save yourself." But she refused to leave me behind. I was terribly ill; I vomited and had a bad case of diarrhea and stomach cramps. Obviously there was nothing to alleviate my pain and sickness, not even water. Ethel managed to find a few girls who were willing to literally drag me on for a while. They did not allow me to stop.

I was very lucky. Shortly after crossing the Elbe bridge (which, by the way, was later demolished by the German soldiers to prevent the approaching Allied forces from crossing the river), we stopped for the night at a country silo. The rest stop, which could not have come too soon as far as my condition was concerned, gave me the necessary time to recover. I spent most of the night vomiting, with diarrhea, but by morning I felt better and my life was saved. That was the only instance I can clearly remember when I had given up hope and was ready to accept the worse. In other difficult situations I had always felt that I wanted to live—feelings so intense that they carried me through the hardships, allowing me, somehow, to survive.

Later, we discovered that the meat that caused my illness was horse-meat. It was the flesh of the horses that had been killed by the bomb blast during the previous day. The girls who gave us the meat happened to be marching near the front of the line and were able to cut some pieces of meat off the horses.

One time, I saw several girls running into an open cellar to get something. I did not know what it was, but I joined them. After descending about ten steps, I saw that they were grabbing cabbages and beets. I do not know how the cellar door happened to be open, but by the time I reached the place there were at least twenty girls there. I, too, grabbed a cabbage head and about four beets and started to run up the steps. Suddenly I saw a German soldier facing me at the top of the stairs with his legs spread apart, holding his rifle in both hands across his waist. He began beating up all the girls ahead of me, as they were coming out. He was hitting and punching right and left, turning to the side with each motion. I made a mad dash at him and ran straight ahead, directly between his spread-open legs and then out to the safety of the crowd, back in the marchers' line. I considered that day to have been an especially lucky one.

At another time I was not very clever. As we marched, I saw a gate nearby and an open house behind it. I ran quickly straight into the house to look for food. There was no one inside. I found myself in a large room that looked like a kitchen. On a table I saw a big round loaf of bread, some eggs, and a big knife. I called out but there was no answer. I suddenly became terribly frightened. An intense, yet unexplained, fear took hold of me and I quickly dashed out of the house without taking anything! All along, I had my blanket with me and I could have taken the entire loaf of bread or, at least, I could have cut off a piece of it with the knife! I could have grabbed the eggs, but I ran out of the house empty-handed! When I returned to the line and told my sisters what had happened, they became very angry. They told me that I was stupid. To this day I am still mad at myself for not taking some of that precious food.

After marching on, we stopped for the night in a town called Bruno. We were to spend the night in several occupied school buildings, where we found bunk beds and various small items scattered around, including some scissors and knives. There was no one about the place and we did not know to whom these items might have belonged. We all started to grab things. All that Ethel and I were able to find was a girdle, but it was a small size and it fit Ethel and helped keep her warm.

The next morning we were joined by a group of about five hundred Russian and Polish women. We did not know whether they were Jewish or not, but we knew that they were Communists, and therefore opposed to the Nazis. From the little that I could understand, these women's fate had not been as bad as ours. They were forced to work in factories and had been living in the school buildings that we had occupied for the night. They had adequate daily food rations and were allowed to keep their hair long, to wear their own clothes and to own some possessions. We realized that the items we took had probably belonged to them. We rationalized that the whole thing did not matter much anyway, because on that day they were forced to join us on the death march. They were not permitted to take anything with them.

After joining us, these women did not intermingle with us much because we did not speak each other's language. Besides, we looked terrible, especially compared to them. Most of us were Hungarians and there were some Belgian and a few French women. Very few of us could speak a Slavic language.

As we walked one day, one of these Russian women suddenly ran out of line as if she had gone crazy. The soldiers brought her back forcibly and one of them shot her to death on the spot, in front of all of us. He used her as an example to terrorize us and as a reminder of what would happen to those who might decide to escape.

Another escape was later attempted by the women who joined us in Bruno. We were marching along a thickly forested highway when we were ordered to stop because German soldiers wanted to rest. We had to remain on the ground, but we were allowed to get up and walk a short distance away to relieve ourselves. The soldiers usually sat, with their guns in their hands, and kept a close look on those who walked away. At one point, six women walked into the forest looking as if they were going to relieve themselves. They were beautiful girls, with long hair and nice clothes. Slowly, they kept walking farther and farther away and then, suddenly, they broke into a run. The soldiers noticed. They got up in a hurry and began to chase the escaping girls, shouting at them to stop. The girls kept on running, but the German soldiers caught up with them quickly and brought them all back. They stood the captured escapees in front of the group and forced them to remove their shoes and coats. Without any hesitation or deliberation they then shot all six of them to death. As they collapsed, the soldiers shot them again. These women, too, served as an example for the rest of us; a reminder of what the soldiers told us would happen to those who tried to escape. It was a very sad episode for us to witness and, of course, it frightened us even more. It brought on more worry and anxiety about our plans to help Miriam and Irene escape. We knew, however, that we had to try an escape, despite the tremendous fear and trepidation.

Later on, we found the opportunity. As we walked, we noticed an open gate nearby. I watched one guard, Ethel watched the other, and then we quickly pushed Miriam and Irene in and through the gate. We just kept on walking. Everything happened so quickly. We did not have time to even say good-bye or anything else, let alone to give them a hug or a kiss. We immediately reorganized our line to include, once again, five people, to conceal the vacated spots. We just kept on walking as if nothing had happened.

We spent that night in another silo. Ethel and I cried. We did not know what would happen to Miriam and Irene. We were concerned and frightened. At the same time we were hopeful. We thought that at least now they had a chance to survive. We had witnessed too many people shot and killed simply because they were unable to go on. We even saw one girl, an acquaintance from our hometown lose her life to exhaustion. She was with her sister, and she was physically strong. But she reached a stage of complete fatigue and collapsed. As the guard raised his rifle to shoot her she cried out to us, "Remember my memorial day when you get home." We could not live with the thought of seeing Irene suffer the same fate.

On the next morning, Ethel and I were still very depressed. As we merged into our line, we looked up and could not believe our eyes: Miriam and Irene were getting into the line with us! We were so happy to see them! We hugged and kissed them repeatedly. We were so worried about them!

We were eager to know how they ended up back in the line with us. They told us that immediately after being pushed through the gate they sneaked into the barn. The owner of the house, however, noticed them as they entered his barn. Along with his wife, the homeowner brought them into their house and offered them food. He also allowed them to wash up. Then he told them that he was very sorry but he could not let them stay because he was too frightened of getting caught harboring Jews. If caught hiding them it would mean sure death to him and his wife, he said. So, early the next morning he handed the two to the guards, who ordered them back to our group.

The German guards did not punish Miriam and Irene because we had entered a large and populated town and it would have looked very bad to execute them there. Miriam and Irene had quickly mixed in with the group, hoping that the guards would not remember who they were and later seek to make an example of them, too. After this escape attempt we did not want to risk our lives again; at least not for a while. We decided to wait for the right opportunity before we tried again. We settled back into our daily routine for several more weeks.

In our second attempt to help Miriam and Irene escape, the situation was similar to the first time. As we marched through a village, we pushed the two through an open gate and behind a fence. It was a brisk operation. Once again, it happened very quickly. This time our ways parted. We did not know what happened to my sister and niece until the end of the war.

Following the escape, Ethel and I were left to continue on the "Death March." We continued to struggle daily, every hour and every minute, to survive. Sometimes, when we reached a brook, the Germans allowed us to stop while they ate and drank. We saw them eat, but we had nothing. We drank water from the brook, or ate the snow we found along our way. The guards ate bacon, pickles and bread. They never shared any food with us. While eating or resting, they always kept their rifles by their feet to deter us from attempting escape.

Meanwhile, we tried to take advantage of the pause in the march. When stopped by the water we immediately removed our clothes and washed them quickly. We constantly fought a battle to keep relatively free of lice. Some people did not care and just let the lice multiply. Their clothes looked alive. Some people removed their clothing one garment at a time and tried to pick out and get rid of all the lice and eggs by hand. Others, including us, washed our clothes every time we could in attempts to remove the eggs and lice. If the sun was out, we dried the clothes by wearing them on our heads or backs. Sometimes we put the wet clothes back on, but that felt cold and, obviously, we never had towels or anything else to dry ourselves with.

We did not have the faintest idea of where we were, or which way we were going. We did not think about looking at the sun to determine our direction. It just was not of any importance to us. We were constantly engrossed in our battle to stay alive. In any case, we did not feel that it would do us any good to know our location, as we were not free to go where we wanted, anyway. We always looked, however, for written signs and clues. I speak four different languages: Romanian, Hungarian, English and Yiddish. When someone spotted a sign and was unable to decipher it, word was quickly passed through the lines until someone was found who could translate it. In this way we managed to learn the names of some towns that we had passed through. As was mentioned earlier, the Germans tried to keep us away from large cities, but sometimes they had no choice. One such city was Dresden.

It was springtime as we approached Dresden, a large city. We thought that it was strange that we saw no people. As we entered the city we saw, to our disbelief, that the sidewalks were covered with food. Everything we could imagine and dream of was right in front of us, in the downtown area; raw and cooked potatoes, apples and many other foods! We reasoned that the inhabitants of Dresden must have seen the marching groups that had preceded us and saw our group approaching as well. They must have been terribly horrified, or frightened, for they had abandoned the streets, moved indoors and drawn the curtains shut. All the city people were well out of sight, hiding inside the homes for fear of being blamed for feeding us. Of course we instantly turned uncontrollable as we attacked the wealth of food. Everyone ran as fast as possible to grab whatever was within reach. In our unstoppable excitement, hunger and eagerness, we trampled and knocked down at last half of the food piles. The soldiers did not know what to do. They were confused. They began to shoot their guns up into the air. They did not dare shoot us in the middle of the city, as their instructions were, probably, to avoid such acts in populated areas. We, however, became very frightened at the sound of the gunshots. Everyone grabbed whatever they could and ran as fast as possible. The Germans then quickly herded us out of the city. That event was one of the very few instances in which people displayed kindness and concern for our suffering. Of course, we did not see even a single one of them.

Having gone through hardships and painful experiences, we were far from what normal people under normal circumstances would be. In our constant attempts to survive and continue on, we had developed certain perceptions and insights. We could even tell, a day or two in advance, who was going to die. It was clear from the look in their eyes. They had a glassy, hollow gaze and we knew that they had given up inside themselves and lost hope. We tried to talk to these poor people, expressing hope, confidence and other positive thoughts. "Just hold on. Soon we'll be stopping somewhere. We'll have a good rest and maybe we'll find some food in the silos," we used to tell them, trying to uplift their spirits. If we could get them to hold on for the rest of the day, we knew that they might have a slight chance of survival. We hoped that once we rested for the night and, possibly, had some food, we could wake up the next morning and cope a little while longer. We believed that there was strength in numbers.

One night we smelled the aroma of fresh baked bread. We also heard some women whispering and saying, "Shhh, shhhh!" My sister said, "Something is going on here!" We felt our way around the darkened silo until we found half a loaf of bread. Somehow, more loaves were coming in through the window! It appeared that the girls had smelled the freshly baked bread, located the source of the smell, climbed on each other's shoulders, broken a glass window and found the bread. Then they got hold of several loaves and passed them through the broken window. This was real bread, of the variety that was reserved strictly for the Nazi soldiers. Ethel and I started to eat the bread instantly, but I said, "Let's not eat it all now. Let's save some of it for tomorrow morning." Ethel said, "No, let's just eat it up now because there might be trouble about this tomorrow. Let's just eat it now."

As Ethel had predicted, as soon as the silo was opened the next morning to let us out, the first thing the guards did was to order us to place all our belongings by our feet. They searched through everything and those who had some bread among their possessions were marched away. Then we heard gunshots. They shot them! We knew that death was their punishment for having taken the bread. This knowledge was confirmed later by a woman who had been among those taken away. Somehow, she was returned to our group. She told us that the women were forced to dig their own graves and then they were shot and fell into the graves. When she heard the shots, she jumped into the grave she had dug and pretended to have died. Later, the Germans captured her somewhere, as she tried to escape. They did not realize that she was one of the "bread thieves." She was brought back to join us on our march. Needless to say, we felt very lucky that we had followed Ethel's suggestion rather then mine.

We were constantly confused by the Germans' inconsistency. As time went on, they became very unpredictable. At times they shot those who could no longer march. At other times they shot the escapees while at other times they let the captured escapees rejoin the rest of the prisoners. I assume that some of them had become tired of the killing and wished that they themselves could escape. They must have known, in the spring of 1945, that the war was nearing its end, and for that reason, they carried their civilian clothes in their knapsacks on their backs. They must have been worried about saving their own skins when it would be known that the Germans had lost the war.

# Photographs

*My mother, Freida Safar*

*Myself in Satu-Mare, 1940*

*Helen Safar and Joe Farkas,*
*our engagement in Satu-Mare, 1940*

*Myself in 1942*

*My brothers Nathan and Andor, 1943*

*My sister Miriam and her daugher, Irene*

*Joe and I, 1943*

*Above: Ethel, Bandi, and Annie.*
*Right: Ethel and Gyurika, 1943*
*Below: Ethel, Bandi, and*
*Gyurika— their last time*
*together before Bandi was sent to*
*the labor camp.*

*Ethel and I with an American G.I. in Susice, May 1945.*
*The G.I. was of Hungarian descent,*
*and spoke with us in Hungarian.*

*Ethel (left) and I, our passport photos upon our return from*
*Susice after the war, July 1945.*
*Our heads had been shaved in the unknown camp,*
*but had grown out since March.*

*Our daughter, Amber,*
*and granddaughter, Kailei*

*Joe and I, 1990*

# CHAPTER 10

# Escape

As time went on and as there seemed to be no hope for us, we had no idea of how the war was going or who the victor was going to be. Ethel and I had decided that we could not go on anymore and that we had to do something. It was the end of April when we reached the decision to try an escape. We did not know Miriam's and Irene's whereabouts, and there were only the two of us to be responsible for. We knew that some people had succeeded in their escape attempts, because our group was constantly shrinking. The sad truth was that our numbers had dwindled mostly because of many deaths, but some people had managed to simply disappear.

One night we stopped to sleep on a hilltop covered with snow. The weather was dreadful; it was raining, thundering, and hailing. The German soldiers pitched their tents and issued us the usual warning about staying in one place and refraining from sitting up, getting up, or moving about. The penalty for such violation was death by shooting, they said. Ethel and I lay side by side in the snow and talked about how we might be able to get away. We decided to conceal our plans and not tell anyone, not even the girl with whom we had been walking, because we realized that a large number of escapees would significantly increase the probability of being captured. Everyone was exhausted as usual and people around us fell asleep very quickly. When it was very quiet and it appeared that everyone was asleep, we started to crawl on our stomachs slowly, down toward the back side of the hill. After a while, at one point, the slope of the hill became somewhat steep and we started to roll too fast. We rolled into a water stream at the bottom of the hill. It was only about a foot deep. We made quite a lot of noise as our feet hit some rocks at the bottom of the stream, and we were concerned that the guards might have heard us. We instantly froze for several minutes and tried to remain as quiet as we possibly could. We listened intently for sounds indicating that someone might be alerted and was coming after us. After a while, since we heard nothing, we started to feel our way about, slowly and cautiously. It was very dark and there was just a sliver of moon visible above us. We proceeded downward, along the stream and away from the hill. Once we were some distance away, we began to move faster. It was a very cold night, and we had been soaking wet from the rain and the stream. Moving fast helped us keep warm.

We were in a frenzy to get as far away as possible. We had spotted a small structure in the distance. As we approached what appeared to be a house, we saw that it was actually a tool shed. We reached the shed quickly and tried to get inside. Unfortunately, there was a lock on the door. We looked for a way to enter and found a wooden window. We pulled on the window and, to our surprise, it opened rather easily. We crawled inside and began to feel our way around. We hoped to find something to eat, but there was no food inside. The shed contained work tools, such as saws and axes and a large bench. Our first concern was to get rid of the letters K.L. (*Koncentration Lager*), painted on the backs of our clothes. The letters were painted with white oil paints and were almost a foot in height, clearly visible from a distance. To be seen with these identifying marks on our clothes would have been certain disclosure of who we were and where we came from. Among the tools, we found a wire-bristled brush, which we used to scrape off most of the painted letters. We also had in our possession a small pair of manicure scissors, which we had obtained in the camp, as well as a blanket given to us in Purskau. Using the scissors, we cut the blanket into two-triangle shaped shawls. We then hung these makeshift garments over our shoulders and backs in an attempt to conceal some of the white lettering traces which we could not fully remove. Our next priority was sustenance. Since we found no food, nor did we have any in our possession, we gathered some snow off the ground outside and melted it for drinking.

During our second night inside the tool shed, we were awakened to the sound of rattling, which came from the lock, outside the door. It was dark and we could not see much. Some light entered the darkness through the cracks between the wall planks. We watched quietly and with much apprehension. We saw a man wearing striped clothing—the same uniform as that which the men had worn in Auschwitz. We were very frightened! We had not seen a male prisoner since we were taken off the cattle cars, upon our arrival in Auschwitz. When in Purskau we heard the beautiful singing voices of the Italian prisoners, but we never saw them. We sat very quietly, waiting to see what would happen. The man walked around but was unable to enter through the door. He then tried the window. He pulled at the window in one direction only and did not succeed. He gave up and walked away.

After three nights in the same place we became terribly hungry. We knew that we could not stay in the shed any longer. We had to go out and somehow find food. Early the next morning, we left the shed and started to walk. After a short while, we reached the outskirts of a village. We were lucky because earlier that morning, the peasants had left some cooked potatoes and corn meal mush for the chickens. We stole the food and ate it. For us, the taste was wonderful, even though it contained neither salt nor spices. We decided to avoid the village until after sunset and enter later, under the cover of darkness. We did not want to stand out and call attention to ourselves. We did not have the vaguest idea where we were. We did not know whether we were in Germany, Czechoslovakia, or Poland. We did not understand any of the Slavic languages and were unable to decipher any of the road signs.

As we walked along the highway toward the town, we slipped away into hiding whenever we saw men or military personnel. At one point we saw a peasant woman wearing a black scarf, accompanied by a man who also wore peasant clothing. They approached us from the direction of the village and as they moved closer toward us we heard that they were speaking Hungarian. We were very surprised to hear our language in the middle of nowhere and we asked them, "Are you Hungarian?" They replied that they were and asked us if we were Hungarian as well. We said that we were and we entered into conversation with them, asking them many questions. There was so much that we wanted and needed to know and they appeared to have such information. From this encounter, we learned that they had fled Hungary, along with the German soldiers, when the Russian army advanced and invaded that part of the country. They had escaped to Breslau and were both working in a factory. When Breslau was bombed, they fled, once again, along with the Germans. They described the terrifying bombing and how they had joined the Germans, attempting to reach the border with Czechoslovakia and cross over to safety. They had heard about a schoolhouse there that was being used as a camp for displaced Hungarians, and were seeking refuge there.

They, too, asked us many questions, for example, where our parents were. We were so emaciated that they mistook us for children of much younger age. We made up a story on the spot, telling them that we too worked in a factory in Breslau, that we had lost our parents and family in the bombings there and that we were lost and wandering about, looking for other Hungarians to stay with. We asked them to tell us where the school was so that we too could go there for shelter and refuge. They instructed us how to get there and we thanked them and said that we would probably see them there. We said good-bye to them, departed, and proceeded to work out a plan of action.

Our plan was to, first of all, try to find a place of shelter for the night, in a house where there would be no men. We assumed that women would be more compassionate and would tend to ask fewer questions. We were extremely concerned with the possibility that a man would turn us in to the town police. Worse yet, we were worried that we might be turned over to the Nazis. The next step in our plan was to find the schoolhouse the Hungarians had told us about. There, we hoped, we would be able to communicate freely in Hungarian and blend in with the crowds.

When we reached the village we tried, very discreetly, to look through the windows, to see who was inside. In one house we saw a tall young woman lighting an oil lamp, as there was no electricity at all. Behind her we saw an older woman. We decided that this might be the right house in which to try to find refuge. We knocked at the door. When the door was opened, we asked in the broken German that we spoke, "May we come in to warm up? We are very cold." The women allowed us in and shared with us the little food that they had. It was corn meal, made with a little bit of milk, water and salt. As we ate they saw how hungry we were and they offered us more, which we gladly accepted.

After we ate, they asked many questions about us. We told them our well-rehearsed fictional story about being Hungarians, on our way to Czechoslovakia, in search of the school where we were to be housed. The women offered to let us sleep in their house for the night as we had hoped that they would. They told us that the border was about ten kilometers away. The younger woman offered us a bed in the middle of the room. Their house had two rooms. They lived in one room and kept the door to the other room closed, in order to conserve heat. As the young woman made our bed we looked at the sight with admiration; it was so beautiful and clean. We had forgotten the beauty of such apparently simple things. Ethel and I kept looking at each other. We had the same thing on our minds; we had to tell them that we had lice.

We then said, "We appreciate this beautiful bed so very much, but we can't sleep in it because we have lice and we would feel very bad if we contaminated your house with lice." The two women were indeed very kind and compassionate. They gained our trust, and we became confident that they would not turn us to the authorities. We decided to tell them everything—the whole truth; and we did. We told them we lied, that we were not from Breslau and that we were Jews who had escaped from the Death March.

They seemed very interested and asked us to tell them more about ourselves and what we had been through. We stayed up until the early morning hours, telling them what we had gone through. As we told them our story they put our clothes in a big pot of boiling water to kill the lice. They also brought in a large bathtub and filled it with soap and hot water. Then they proceeded to scrub and clean us thoroughly. We did not have much hair, but the older woman, nevertheless, brought in a container filled with kerosene and scrubbed our scalps to get rid of the lice. When they saw our bodies, they both cried, because they felt very sorry for us. We must have looked truly pitiful. We were nothing but skin and bones.

These two kind women then showed us to the bed and told us not to worry about anything. The older woman said that her daughter would escort us across the border the next night. She knew the area well and knew exactly where the guards and sentries were positioned to check the documents of those who wanted to cross the border. We, of course, did not have any legal papers. We slept better that night than we had in a very long time.

The next morning, the women went outside to get our clothes, which were hanging out to dry, but the garments had frozen solid and we could not leave for at least a while. We were concerned because we did not want to put these women in jeopardy for harboring us. In the event that we were recognized for who we really were, the women could have suffered severe negative consequences for providing us shelter and food. The two opened the back room in their house and started a fire in the stove. They then hung our clothes above, to dry. We spent the rest of the day inside the second room. Our generous hosts came in occasionally throughout the day, bringing food and drink. They also continued to talk and listen to us as they were very interested to hear more about our experiences. They were truly shocked and horrified by all that had become of us. We also learned a few things about them. The older woman was Czechoslovakian and her husband was German. We were now in Germany, very near the Czech border. The younger woman was her daughter who, in the social terminology of the time, was considered to be an "old maid" because she had passed the expected marriage age without ever finding a mate. As far as we were concerned, some man would have been truly fortunate, for she had a heart of gold and the soul of a saint.

A day later, our clothes were dry. The women gave us some underwear and more clothes to keep us warm. That night the daughter walked us across the border. We said good-bye and gave many thanks, and we swore that if we were to remain alive, we would come back someday with gifts for them to try, somehow, to repay them for their kindness. We had developed a mutual kinship.

# CHAPTER 11

# After the Escape

When we arrived at the schoolhouse, we were still very frightened. We decided that only one of us should go into the office, so that if some problem were to arise, only one of us would be affected while the other could escape. We determined that Ethel would wait outside. I walked in and said that I had just arrived from Breslau, pretending to be a Hungarian Nazi sympathizer. I repeated the story that we had heard from the peasant couple we had met on the road. They asked me what my name was and I revealed my maiden name, which did not sound like a Jewish name. They instructed me to sign a document of registration. I told them my sister had been waiting outside because she had to go to the bathroom. They just told us, "Go up to the second floor. There's an empty corner in the classroom where you can stay." They issued us tickets which we could use for food downstairs in the dining room. We threw away our coats, on which the huge letters K.L. were still faintly visible.

We immediately walked downstairs to eat. The food tasted wonderful! We were so hungry that we went back for second and third helpings! We tried to hide the fact that we were so starved, but it must have been rather obvious to anyone observing us.

We pretended to be poor, simple and helpless girls. Most of the other residents of the schoolhouse did not eat the food offered in the dining room. They did not consider it to be as tasty and good as we did. Instead, many of them preferred to eat in nearby restaurants.

We discovered that it was rather easy to avoid being exposed as Jews. We spoke fluent Hungarian, which was our mother tongue, and people had no reason to doubt our story. The war was almost over by that time, and they probably did not pay much attention to or care much about who we were. In fact, no one ever checked our identity, nor were we ever summoned to the officer in charge for questioning or inquiry. Perhaps, had we been men, we would have been checked out more thoroughly. At the time, only Jewish boys were regularly circumcised after birth and it was rather easy to determine a male's religious affiliation by a simple examination.

In reality, everyone realized that the end of the war was nearing and that it was only a matter of weeks, perhaps just days, before the war would be over. It was clear that the officials in charge were instead carrying on while trying not to be burdened with unnecessary concerns.

Once settled in, we discovered a Hungarian couple seated in one corner of the room surrounded by nine children. Since both Ethel and I have always loved children, we proceeded to help the couple attend to their many offspring. We took them for walks, we played with them, and I remember knitting wool booties for each of the smaller children. They did not like the food which was served in the dining hall, so we cooked them special meals any time the man was able to find different food items. The mother of this family appeared to have lived a very hard and demanding life, and she was clearly resentful of her husband, who had brought them into this predicament by insisting that they, along with all their children, flee in the footsteps of the retreating Germans. We never found out why they had to flee, but it appeared that the husband was afraid of the Russians for one reason or another. It is possible that he had held an official government position, or that he had done something wrong. Despite her bitterness, the woman was very appreciative and grateful for our help, and the two managed to reciprocate in small ways.

We stayed in the schoolhouse for about ten days. On the fifth of May we heard, over the loudspeaker, someone yell *"Pozor! Pozor!"* ("Attention! Attention!") Everyone ran to take a look out of the window. Ethel, too, looked and saw American soldiers marching through the streets. Then she noticed a beautifully dressed officer, getting off an open jeep. He wore a clearly visible Star of David on his cap. We were still concerned about possible danger and were very careful to avoid being identified as Jewish. Although we felt the urge, we did not want to scream out the window that we were Jews. We were not supposed to be Jews; we were pretending to be Hungarian Nazi sympathizers! So we ran downstairs as fast as we could and sought out the officer by his jeep.

In our excitement, we were not certain about what language to use in attempting to communicate with him, so all we said was, *"Mogen David! Mogen David!"* ("Star of David!") Speaking Yiddish, the officer asked us if we knew what it was and we told him, in Yiddish, that we did. We were Jews, we said. He appeared amazed and asked us what we were doing there. We began to tell him of our ordeal. While we were outside talking to him, the Czechs were locking up the school building, to assure that no one would get out. They already had their rifles on their shoulders. All the Hungarian Nazi sympathizers in the school were now destined to go to prison. The officer told us that he was the chaplain of the U.S. regiment, which was the first to occupy the area. He said that he would take care of us, but we could no longer stay in the school building. He gave us some chocolate, cigarettes, and beautiful soft white bread, the like of which I had never seen before. He instructed us to wait as he approached the locked-up schoolhouse and deleted our names from the list of occupants. His action assured that we would not be taken away with the other prisoners. He also went upstairs and gathered our meager possessions.

He said that he was sorry because he had to move on with the military troops, but he handed us over to the Czech mayor of the town, Susice Nad/Sumavow. He assured us that the mayor would take good care of us and would help us move out of the town. The Nazis had occupied the mayor's house, but with the Allies' liberation he was reinstated to his official position. The mayor put us up in his house and invited us to stay there and make ourselves at home. He had to leave in search of his family, to find out whether or not his wife was still alive. She was Jewish and had been taken to the Theresienstadt concentration camp. Later, he found her alive and brought her back home.

We stayed with the mayor and his wife for six weeks. We never had any money throughout our entire stay, nor did we need any. Our hosts bought us everything we could possibly need, including new clothes and shoes, suits, food and other necessities and little luxuries. They also helped me with important medical care. I had acquired a staph infection while in the school building and had boils covering my entire body, including my bottom. I could not sit down for weeks. I also had boils inside my ears, severely interfering with my hearing. The mayor and his wife took me to the military hospital in town, where I received the proper injections and underwent treatment for about a month.

One day, while we were at the mayor's home, he approached us and said, "Come with me." He took us to a prison building, where in one of the cells was a young man of about twenty-five. He was a good looking S.S. military man, covered with black and blue marks, sustained while having been seriously beaten up. He sat in a corner of the cell and appeared clearly frightened. The mayor said that we could do anything we wanted to him. He suggested that we could hit him, kick him, spit on him, abuse him...whatever we wanted. My sister and I just looked at each other and we said, "No". Then we walked out. We had seen enough suffering. The Czechs were very bitter and revengeful. They imprisoned many Nazis and punished them whenever they could. This Nazi prisoner was the only one we saw after the war.

On one occasion, we returned to the schoolhouse to visit the family we had cared for, with their many children. When those staying at the building found out that we were Jewish they seemed shocked! Many of them asked us to bring them various things from the town. Once, during another visit, we brought some items for the children, but we never went back again.

The mayor and his wife took care of us and gave us many gifts. These included china and crystal items that the German soldiers had left behind in his home. We took as many of these presents as we could carry and then looked up the two women, the mother and her daughter, who had taken care of us earlier and helped us get across the border. We found them where we left them, in their home, and we gave them all the presents. We never found out what their names were, nor did they know our names. We were always so preoccupied with other burning concerns, such as food and survival, that it just never occurred to us to ask.

The mayor and his wife wanted very much to adopt us. The wife had asked us to stay with them and she promised to help us find men to marry. She advised us not to go home because there was probably no one still alive. It would be a sad and useless experience, she said, to return to our hometown. It was then, for the first time, that we revealed to a stranger that Ethel was a married woman whose young son was killed in Auschwitz. We told the woman that we had to go home to look for and find whoever was still alive. We wanted to find our homes, too.

The mayor and his wife helped us obtain travel documents and permits. They took us to the appropriate offices and spoke their native Czech language as they arranged all the necessary details on our behalf. They took full responsibility for us and testified under oath that we were not subversive. They secured all the necessary documents for us. These papers were extremely important to us. They represented our regained identities. The documents were far more important than food, for at that time in war-torn Europe, one could hardly move about without being frequently stopped and asked to produce identification or travel documentation.

Finally it was time for us to leave. We thanked our generous and caring hosts and said good-bye. We were about to begin our long journey home.

# CHAPTER 12

# The Journey Home

We started out from Susice by train. Because of the war, however, train tracks had been either destroyed or damaged. Consequently, we could not simply take a train ride directly to our destination. Instead, at times, we had to detour impassable areas and go a long way out of our intended route. Frequently, we had to sit inside the train-car for days, inside train stations, waiting anxiously to catch a train headed north, to Romania. (After the war, Stalin handed Transylvania back to the Romanians, so the border had moved once again and our hometown was now a part of Romania.) We constantly tried to associate with and befriend other families who traveled in the same direction, because we had neither money nor food. We offered to help care for their children, which provided us opportunities to earn a little bit of food for ourselves. We also wanted companionship, and the association with others while we traveled was important. Often we had to plan our journey and we helped each other to figure out where we were and where we were going.

At one time, I remember, we had found a train filled with Polish and Slovak people. We did not have much understanding of Slovak languages, but we managed to ask them if we could join them on the train. We explained to them in what direction we intended to travel. After some broken discussion one of the passengers finally said, "All right, come!" We boarded the train, which was already very crowded. Before we even had an opportunity to settle down, some people began to shout, "Out! Out!" and before we understood what had happened we were ejected. We could not understand why we were rejected in such a blunt manner. As we stood there, watching the train leave, we suddenly realized that it was going in a different direction from our intended destination.

At another time, we traveled on flat-bed train-cars. At that stage of the war, the Russians were busily collecting jeeps and other vehicles for shipment back to their country. The Russians referred to this activity as *zabra*, which, very loosely translated, means stealing from occupied areas. We approached a Russian officer positioned by one of the freight trains and asked him if we could possibly get on the train and just sit there with the jeeps. We tried to explain to him that we were Jewish refugees trying to get back to our homes. We hoped that he would be sympathetic and would let us board. The train had been parked there for a little while, and the officer agreed to let us get on.

We boarded the train and sat down. We were able to carry on some conversation with the man. Using some of the little German we knew and with some Yiddish, we were able to tell him a little about what we had experienced in Auschwitz and the other troubles that we had undergone. We spent most of that day with him and he showed a great deal of interest and sympathy. Indeed, he seemed to feel very sorry for us. At one point he left and returned a short while later with some food. He brought us very good black bread, bacon, and pickles and we all ate together. When nightfall approached, he informed us that we could sleep in one of the jeeps which had been loaded on the train. We were so happy! In the vehicle it was warm because it was covered with a tarp. We were elated because we realized that we were on board a train that was heading in the right direction.

During that night we were suddenly startled to discover that someone had dropped into the jeep from above! It was dark and the man tried to rape Ethel! It turned out to be the sympathetic Russian officer who had allowed us to get onto the train! Ethel had told him earlier that she had lost her child and that she did not know whether or not her husband was alive. The Russian had probably concluded that she was an easy target of whom he could take advantage. We became very frightened. Ethel, the fast thinker as she was, began saying and repeating, *"Ich hab' Syphilis!"* ("I have syphilis!") This frantic warning was apparently sufficient to ward off the attacker. The officer changed his mind very quickly and left in the same manner in which he had entered.

The next morning, the Russian officer seemed to have forgotten his previous night's activity. He pretended that nothing out of the ordinary had happened. Possibly, he may have concluded that we did not know that he was the intruder. We, too, preferred to pretend that we did not suspect him, realizing that we were at his mercy and aboard the train because of him. We spent only that single night on the train and went nowhere. Later, the officer told us to get off the train because it was headed in the wrong direction.

So once again we had no choice but to wait. At one point during that time we met some people from our hometown, and we all joined together in our hope to move on. One of the men in this group was, too, a survivor of a concentration camp. He took special care of us, treating us in a very father-like fashion, as if we were his daughters. He ran from train to train, asking questions in an attempt to find the right train for us to take us home. He spoke some Russian and was able to communicate better than we. He was with us throughout the rest of our journey, accompanying us all the way home, to Satu-Mare.

# CHAPTER 13

# Arriving Home

We arrived in Satu-Mare on a Sunday. Joe, my fiancé, was a center-forward for the Sanitas, the local Jewish soccer team. He was to participate in a soccer match on that day. We had been engaged before the war, but I assumed that he thought I was dead.

Joe's best friend, Alex Grunfeld, went to the train station every day, hoping that his sisters, Elza and Sari, would return. Alex did not have a father, and he knew that since his sisters and his mother were sent to Auschwitz together, his mother could not have lived, but he continued to hold some hope that his sisters might have survived. He showed up at the train station daily, hoping to see them return. We, of course, knew the unfortunate fate of his sisters. On the death march, Elza had sustained the head affliction that had probably caused her death, while Sari died later of starvation in the unnamed camp.

When we arrived home we found Alex waiting at the train station. Obviously, he was very happy to see us alive. He took us, by horse and carriage, to the apartment that he had been sharing with Joe. All my furniture, as well as other items that had been part of my dowry, were there, including the linen which my parents had bought us in anticipation of our coming marriage. I had given these items to my friend Julia, who was not Jewish, just before we were sent off to the ghetto. When Joe returned from the forced-labor camp, she gave it all back to him.

They had employed a maid who took care of the house, and she immediately prepared some food for us, and we were able to take a bath. While we were getting cleaned up, Alex rushed to the soccer field and, in the middle of the game, excitedly told Joe that his fiancée and her sister had finally returned home! Joe literally abandoned the ball and the game and headed home as quickly as he could, arriving to meet us still wearing his sweaty soccer uniform.

Joe and Alex had been liberated from the forced-labor camp after the arrival of Russian troops, in September 1944. The Russians placed them on a truck headed for Kolosvar, with the intention of taking them to Russia as prisoners, but the two were able to jump off the vehicle, escape and hide. They walked a distance of almost 300 kilometers (approximately 200 miles) until finally, after a slow and tedious journey, they reached home, in Satu-Mare. The two had arrived at about the time the Russian military forces were in the process of occupying the territory. Confusion and chaos characterized the situation.

Other Jewish survivors had just begun to arrive home, seeking to restore their lives and to find remnants of their prewar belongings. In his search, Joe went to the different homes in which members of my family used to live, but was able to retrieve almost nothing, as these places had been looted. Almost everything was taken away. He did, however, find my younger brother Nathan there. When Joe arrived, Nathan was asleep on a stack of straw which served as his bed. Nathan told Joe that he was about to join a Zionist group and that he planned to go to Palestine.

Later, Joe and Alex were able to realize their claim on the apartment and move in. They tried to bring their lives back to a level of normalcy, but things were never the same as they had been. At least, they rationalized, they had regained their freedom. They were obviously concerned and hopeful, at the same time, as they anxiously waited to find out who survived and was able to return home.

Susice was liberated on May 5, when the American soldiers marched in. Ethel and I arrived home in the middle of July; so it had taken us about two and a half months to reach our hometown.

Joe and I were married on August 4, 1945. I sold the home that my parents had built because after it was ravaged by war, hardly anything was left of it. Everything was stolen, even the windows and floors.

It was extremely difficult for Ethel to regain possession of her parents-in-law's apartment. Life had been chaotic and disorganized while we were away. There was no law and order enforced, and people simply moved into dwellings that seemed unoccupied or abandoned. It was a squatter's paradise. For many people the ability to physically occupy a place was equivalent to gaining ownership rights to it. With time and with the help of her landlord, Ethel finally managed to gain access to her in-laws' apartment and move in. Her brother-in-law moved in as well. She did not know at the time that her husband, Bandi, was alive. Years later, in the summer of 1948, he suddenly appeared, after having been taken prisoner by the Russians. While her husband was missing, Ethel had frequently been offered marriage, but she kept refusing her suitors, insisting, "I still have the feeling that my husband is alive.... I'll just wait." In the meantime, in order to earn a living, she rented parts of her apartment, cooked for her boarders and cleaned for them. Bandi had finally come home and by the following winter Ethel was pregnant with her second child, Anna.

My husband Joe and his friend Alex went into business. They opened a shoe store in Satu-Mare, which appeared to be the natural thing to do, since Joe had been trained and had experience in the shoe business before the outbreak of the war. Upon our marriage, Joe and Alex decided to separate and divide their possessions. Joe offered that Alex choose between the shoe store and the apartment, and Alex selected the store. Joe and I remained in the apartment, which was a valuable asset to have in those days, under the post-war conditions. It was very difficult to find a place to rent; the demand was high and the available apartments were extremely difficult to find. We knew we were fortunate and we were very happy newlyweds to be able to enjoy the privacy of our own apartment. Even today, in the 1990s, people in Satu-Mare still live in small, cramped apartments, where several families often crowd within a single dwelling unit.

Later, Joe's siblings came home, too. His brothers Morris and Sol and his sisters Lilly and Rose were among the returnees. Since Joe and I were the only married couple and because we had the good fortune to own our beautiful apartment, they all came to live with us. We had a large living room and they slept on the floor. They stayed with us for about a year until, one by one, they got married and found places of their own.

# CHAPTER 14
# My Family

Many members of my family never returned home because they perished in the Nazi concentration camps. Lost were my parents; Ethel's little boy, Gyurika; my oldest brother, Moshe, his wife and two children; my sister Regina, her husband, their three children, and her husband's entire family; and my brother Andor.

Andor died after we were separated in Auschwitz. Dr. Mengele gathered about 2,000 young teenage boys, all over the age of seventeen. They were held in the camp and later loaded onto cattle cars and taken away to a large snow-covered field. They had thought that they were to be put to work somewhere, since they were young and strong. Instead, they were all shot *en masse* with machine guns. We knew that this was their fate because one of these young men managed to survive. After his return home, he happened to live next door to where we lived. He had known Andor and was with him in the killing field. The boy survived because, when the machinegun fire began, he fainted, fell down and was left for dead. When he came to his senses, he saw that the German soldiers were examining bodies and shooting anyone who was still moving or appeared to be alive. He held his breath, did not move a muscle and pretended to be dead. Once the German soldiers left, he fainted again. When he was revived for the second time, he found himself on a Russian train, surrounded by Russian soldiers. He also discovered that all his toes were amputated. His toes had been frostbitten and someone had performed surgery on him while he was unconscious. He did not know or remember the ordeal, nor how he ended up on that train. The Russians released him in 1948.

The only other members of my family, other than Ethel and I, to survive the concentration camps were Miriam and Irene. We did not know of their fate until we received a letter from them, addressed to my parents' house in Satu-Mare. The letter was forwarded to us, to our apartment, and we were able to respond. We found out where they were located and we were later reunited. That is when we finally found out what happened to them following their escape.

After we had pushed them through the open fence, Miriam and Irene made their way to a nearby barn. Once inside, they climbed over some animals, up to the hay loft and hid in the haystacks. They found some sugar beets that had been provided for the animals, which they ate.

The following morning, the farmer climbed up to the loft to get some hay for the animals. Miriam suddenly had a strong urge to sneeze and was unable to restrain herself. The farmer heard the sound and asked, "Who's there?" The two were much too frightened to answer. Realizing that someone was hiding in the haystack, the farmer began to stab his pitchfork into the hay, in an effort to force the fugitives out. As he was getting dangerously close to stabbing them with the pitchfork, Miriam and Irene were forced to move back. The farmer noticed the motion and discovered them shortly afterwards. So after only one night of freedom, the two were captured and taken to the mayor of the village.

As they waited in his nice, warm office, they were given some food. Then the mayor apologized and told them that, while he regretted it very much, he had no other choice but to turn them over to the Germans. They were to join the next group of prisoners scheduled to pass through the village. They were locked up in the mayor's office for the night and the next morning, when another group came through, they were handed over to the officer in charge.

The group of prisoners was a small one and the *Wehrmacht* was a kind man who referred to them as *"Meine Kinder"* (my children). While our group was forced to march about fifteen to twenty kilometers each day, Miriam and Irene's new group walked about five to eight kilometers daily. The German officer appeared to be rather kind and allowed the marchers to make frequent stops and take adequate time to rest. Later they found out that he had been given orders to take the prisoners to a concentration camp known as Bergen-Belsen. During the night, the German tried to obtain food for his captives. He went through the area villages and asked some of the local citizens to cook potatoes for them. Through his efforts, the prisoners were adequately fed every night. The German officer was never violent and the group members were never punished physically. As a result of his humane treatment, no one attempted to escape. The prisoners had realized that their fate under this man's command was preferable to the much worse circumstances they might have had to endure under someone else.

The German officer delivered the group to Bergen-Belsen, where they remained until finally being liberated.

Following their release, Miriam was hospitalized because she was still infected with typhus. Many people passed through the hospital, and Miriam met an acquaintance who had known Ethel and me. This person told her that Ethel had survived and gone home, but that I had died. Until we were reunited much later, Miriam and Irene were certain that I was no longer alive. When Miriam regained her health and strength, she was released and traveled back home, to Kolosvar. There she remarried, and in 1947 she and her husband, Mishi, emigrated to the city of Haifa, in what became, a year later, the State of Israel.

Irene, my niece, was also married in 1946. Two years later, she gave birth to a son, Chaim, and in January of 1949 they, too, moved to Israel. In 1950, Irene had a girl, Carmella. Eighteen years later, when Chaim for the first time came home wearing the uniform of the Israel Defense Forces, Irene could not contain her emotions, and said, "This is my revenge against the Nazis—to see my own son in the uniform of the Jewish army in an independent Israel." Currently, Irene is a member of a kibbutz in northern Israel. My sister Miriam also lived on the same kibbutz during the last years of her life and passed away in 1982.

My other sister, Lenke, and her husband had been living in Bucharest, Romania before the war. When the war broke out, the Romanians did not surrender the Jewish population to the Germans, to be taken to the camps, as was done by other governments under the German occupation. Instead, they attempted to find and kill the Jews themselves. To gain favor in the eyes of the Germans, the Romanians had "advertised" their deeds by publicizing their atrocities in the press. Thus, for example, Romanian newspapers have published photographs of dead Jews, hanging on butcher-hooks, covered with signs proclaiming, "Kosher

Meat." Non-Jewish Romanians were ordered to post signs in their house-fronts stating "Christian House." Those who were discovered to have harbored Jews had to suffer the consequences. Punishment was certain and the risk was high enough to deter such attempts. Lenke and her husband were very lucky, because their landlord was a very good individual. He had risked his own life by placing a "Christian house" sign in his window, even though he knew that his tenants were Jewish. Their apartment was never searched, and during the short time-period in which Romania purged itself of its Jewish population, they managed to escape detection. Lenke remained in Bucharest even after the war until her husband's death, in the early 1970s. Then she, too, moved to Israel, where she joined Miriam, Irene, and her growing family.

My brother Eddie went to Belgium in the late 1920s and was married there. When the war broke out and the Germans invaded Belgium, Eddie and his wife, Helen, fled to France, riding a motorcycle. As they and thousands of other people were fleeing, German war planes fired at them from the sky. They survived the attacks and later made contact with members of the French underground and joined them in their fight of resistance against the invading Germans. Later they were discovered and captured by the Germans and were jailed.

While they were in jail, a hand grenade was mysteriously tossed into their cell. They did not know, and never did find out, who threw it in. Eddie quickly grabbed the grenade and managed to throw it out of the cell. They heard an explosion. Within minutes, they were removed from their cell and forced to lie down on the floor to be shot. Suddenly they heard gunfire and a great commotion ensued. Eddie, Helen, and the others quickly got to their feet and ran for their lives.

It turned out that the partisans had arrived at the last minute, just before the prisoners were to be executed. The partisans had created a distraction and great confusion and then rescued the prisoners. Rejoining the fighters of the underground resistance, Eddie and Helen fought the Nazis until the end of the war. When the war was over, they returned to Belgium to renew their lives. There, Helen gave birth to a son, Andrei Several years later, they moved to America.

Years earlier, shortly after the Nazi occupation and before our removal to the ghetto, my other brother, Nathan, went to Budapest, using a friend's false documents. There, in the Hungarian capital, he joined Beytar, a Zionist group headed by Menachem Begin, who later led the Jewish underground struggle against the British in Palestine and who, in 1977, was elected to the post of Prime Minister of Israel. Throughout the war years, Nathan was active in Europe, risking his life to save Jews in subversive, anti-Nazi activities. At one time, Nathan and other Beytar members impersonated Nazi S.S. officers and stole several military trucks loaded with food, which they drove into the ghetto to feed the inhabitants. Then they simply disappeared.

At one time the Hungarian Nazis discovered Nathan and another Beytar partner. They had to escape, and as they ran, under extensive gunfire, the friend was shot and killed. Nathan was wounded, suffering several bullet shots in his leg. He managed, however, to hide behind an open door and was not discovered. He carried these bullets in his leg for years. During the war he traveled with the Beytar movement to Italy, France, and Belgium, where he met up with Eddie. Later, he moved to Israel, got married, and had two sons, Avi and Rami. In the 1960s, the family moved to the

United States, where their daughter, Beki, was born. We did not find out about Nathan's heroic wartime activities until after the war, when my girlfriend, a resident of Budapest, told us all about his deeds. Nathan died of diabetes at the age of sixty-nine.

# CHAPTER 15

# After the War

The memory of our lost families was constantly with us. Every step we took and every corner we turned reminded us of their absences. Otherwise, life after the war appeared to be beautiful. Joe and his brother Morris excelled in their business venture and opened a beautiful new shoe store in the downtown area. Before the war Morris had been a traveling salesman who had earned significant income selling hats. He offered his clients the very best merchandise, distinguished for its high quality. As conditions affecting the Jewish population worsened, Morris decided to give up his business. He turned his hat supply over to a close, non-Jewish friend.

When Joe returned home after the war, this friend gave him Morris' stock of hats, which Joe sold to earn income to finance his shoe store. The demand for shoes after the war was very high, and it was rather common to see people wearing wood-soled shoes. First the German occupiers had confiscated everything; later, with Soviet occupation, the Russians had taken anything and everything they could find. Under these conditions the shoe business flourished. Everyone needed shoes, and the two brothers, hardly able to keep up with the demand, experienced difficulties in keeping the store shelves fully stocked! We lived in comfort and we had everything we needed or wanted.

Joe and I were very happy with each other in our marriage. We wanted to have children as soon as possible but I was unable to conceive. We tried to find out what the reason was, but with the state of medical research and knowledge at the time, we had no definitive answers. I tried many different remedies and "cures" in my attempts to become more fertile, but to no avail. It may have been that the problem was a result, or at least related to, the physical and mental hardships, suffering and deprivation of the previous years. Long periods of near-starvation and the drugs that the Nazis had inserted into our meager food portion to curtail menstruation probably had much to do with this problem.

Later I was afflicted with hepatitis. I had cooked a goose the day before, and we did not have proper refrigeration. In order to preserve food for as long as possible and to protect it from spoiling we used to place it in a dark and naturally-cold pantry. As I became hungry, I walked to the pantry, grabbed a goose leg and started eating it in the dark, on my way out. When I entered a lit area, I was able to look at the goose leg, only to discover that it was infested with maggots. I had already taken several bites and the result was a violent illness which led to hepatitis. As it happened, I had finally conceived shortly before this incident. The unfortunate result was miscarriage. I was compelled to spend about two months in bed, and I was yellow with jaundice for a long time.

We lived in Satu-Mare until the end of 1948. With the rapid rise of communism, people began to mysteriously "disappear." The Communist rule turned increasingly strict and restrictive, interfering in our daily lives with growing intensity. Many people, especially those who were not seriously limited or committed to family or work, began to leave, on their way to the newly established State of Israel. Rumors spread, suggesting certain people knew how to escape from behind the Iron Curtain, where we happened to be situated. Others were frequently rounded up and arrested for reasons which appeared to be increasing trivial, insignificant, or for no apparent reason at all. Freedom of speech became non-existent and all but a remote ideal. I knew of a man, a blacksmith, who became intoxicated in a bar and was overheard to say, "I would like to be the man who puts the horseshoes on the horse that carries Stalin's funeral casket." It was a very short while before he was taken away by the authorities, long before he had an opportunity to sober up. It was rumored that he was severely beaten and tortured until he died. The conditions and overall atmosphere had become so repressive and restrictive that one could no longer trust anybody.

In schools, children were taught to tell their teachers what they had overheard at home. It was quite common for young children to divulge information about members of their families, which led to arrest and persecution for crimes of subversion. Many Jews who had not been in their homes long enough to become emotionally attached had decided to leave.

Morris, who was handsome and wealthy at that time, managed somehow to attract the wrong kind of attention. We had discovered, through rumors, "leaks" and word of mouth that his name had been placed on the infamous "black list." This, by all accounts, was an extremely dangerous development which caused us alarm and serious concern. We began to plan our escape from behind the Iron Curtain.

We started out by selling off all the merchandise in the shoe store, but we could not risk it in the open and be obvious about it. So as we sold the shoes, we placed the empty boxes back on the shelves so that the store continued to look well stocked. Joe and Morris converted the money into American dollars through the local black market, which was the only way to obtain foreign currency. Such a transaction constituted a major legal offense, sufficient to land the offender in jail for a long time.

Morris went to someone in an attempt to find information about the possibility of escape. He discovered that a man by the name of Salty owned property across the border with Hungary. He was taking people across the border in exchange for a significant amount of American dollars. If he were to take us across, we would proceed to the Rothschild Center in Vienna, Austria, to arrange passage to either Israel or to the United States.

Ethel was pregnant with Annie at the time, and was not in a position to make the escape journey with us. They all came to the U.S. legally, in 1962, with their daughter, Anna. Ethel's husband, Bandi, had passed away at the age of sixty-four. His early death was partially a result of over six years of imprisonment in Russian concentration camps. Ethel died in 1987 after a long illness, caused by her suffering in the concentration camps. She never got over the loss of her first child, Gyurika.

I was recovering from hepatitis and still very weak, but the time to leave had come. It could well be the last opportunity. It was then or never. We planned the escape very carefully. The plan involved Joe and me; Morris, his wife Lenci, and their fifteen-month-old baby boy, Gabie. There was also another couple with a small boy. They had a truck which was to be used in the escape. It was this man who had put us in contact with Salty earlier. Salty had said that he would take only three couples across at one time. That quota was filled, but we also had two babies to care for!

# CHAPTER 16

# Escape from Communism

I said good-bye to Ethel and Bandi. We gave them the key to our apartment, so that at nightfall they could enter and take whatever they could, without being noticed. The shoe store was not opened the next morning, and government officials immediately began to look for us. As far as we knew, we left no trace. Our apartment was empty and even after thoroughly questioning our relatives, no one knew anything about our whereabouts.

We made our escape on December 28, 1948, which happened to be Morris' birthday. It was a dark and very foggy night. We walked across the bridge of the river Szamos, which flowed within our town. There we met up with the other couple. The two children had been given sleeping suppositories by a discreet and willing doctor, to keep them comfortable and quiet. We rode the other couple's truck until we reached the agreed-upon meeting spot with Salty. There we abandoned the truck on the highway and continued on foot.

We had to walk across the border through the snow and in dense fog. We had brought a sled in which to pull the children in the snow, and the two were heavily bundled up in a papoose made of fur. As we walked through a cornfield, the recently-cut, sharp stalks tore open one of the papooses and the baby woke up and began to cry. His crying awoke the other boy and they both began to cry. We had to abandon the sled and carry the boys in our arms in order to keep them warm and quiet. We had been told to bring a white sheet for each one of us to provide camouflage in the snow, so we were all covered up with those garments. We had also been told to wear a pair of good walking shoes since we were going to walk a great distance. I was unable to obtain the proper footwear at our store, which carried only stylish fashion shoes for women. Nor did we have sufficient time to prepare fully. So I bought a pair of high-top shoes but I did not have any time to break them in. I was not able to use these, for Joe was concerned that they would injure my feet. I ended up using the shoes I had owned—a pair of high heeled sandals which I wore inside a pair of overshoes. It was very difficult for me to walk. Marching through a cornfield, I tripped continuously and fell over the chopped corn stalks. Snow kept getting inside my galoshes.

We did not take many possessions with us. One of our friends made us travel bags with a zipper. In it I put our pajamas, a few clothing items and a pillowcase that I had thought we could fill with clothes to use for a pillow. We did not take anything of value and the only piece of jewelry I had on me was my wedding band.

The three men kept passing the two children back and forth among them, but they were getting tired and the boys seemed to be getting heavier and very difficult to carry. After a while, the truck-owner became too weak to carry his child and Joe carried the boy. The man's wife, who was pregnant, carried a large bundle that, we assumed, contained necessities for their child and the expected baby. Joe and I felt very sorry for the woman and, to help out, Joe carried her bundle on his back whenever he could. At one point, as the walking became more demanding, Lenci threw her purse down in desperation and said that she could not carry it anymore. I picked up the purse and carried it for her. After a little while the pregnant woman's husband sat down in the snow and said, "I'm too tired. I can't go on. Take my wife and child and leave me here." Joe and Morris became extremely angry with him! They tried to convince him to get up and continue. When their persuasive attempts failed, their anger grew and they threatened to use force. They told him, "Snap out of your self pity. Get up and be a man. Your wife is pregnant, yet she is walking. I'm carrying your son. We'll beat the hell out of you if you don't get up and face your responsibilities!" The man finally rose and continued to walk with us.

We were very apprehensive and frightened because we had heard that during the previous night guards had shot five young Jewish men from Satu-Mare as they tried to escape. Salty continuously reminded us to keep the children quiet. We were almost at the border. He kept encouraging us to keep on and to continue walking because we were very close to our destination. Then he suddenly said, "Be very quiet. We're at the border." We were very tense and prayed that the children would not cry. All that while we tried to keep track of each other in the thick fog, which was so dense that we could hardly see a few feet in front of us. All of a sudden the guard dogs began to bark. We heard the guards shout, "*Stai! Stai!*" which, in Romanian, means "stop, stop!" We were alarmed and frightened. The tension and fear were so great that we almost welcomed the possibility of being captured rather than facing the guards' guns and getting shot, as had the men during the previous night.

Luck, however, was with us. The guards must have been either too lazy or too cold to investigate the reasons for the watchdogs' alarm. It was late December, close to New Year's Day. We had chosen what, in retrospect, was a very good time to cross the border. The area was often very foggy and dark and the guards appeared to be preoccupied with maintaining their own comfort, celebrating and drinking in observance of the new year. We continued to walk and the border guards did not pursue us. They probably did not even notice our passage.

We were exhausted after walking through the entire night. I became very weak since I had not had a chance to fully recover from the hepatitis. After walking for some distance beyond the border, Salty instructed us to sit down. He pulled a shot glass from his pocket and a bottle of schnapps, which seemed to appear out of nowhere and he poured the liquor into the tiny glass. We all shared in the drink and rejoiced to celebrate the moment and the successful completion of the adventure. We had made it across the border into Hungary!

Salty brought us to a house where he uttered a password at the entrance. We entered. The house belonged to a local peasant and his wife. They offered us another drink and warm food. Salty said that we needed to give these people something for harboring us and we paid them some money. The pregnant woman in our group opened up the bundle that Joe had carried for her, to offer something to our hosts. As we looked at her bundled possessions we were shocked. We had thought that it contained absolute necessities. Instead, it consisted of dirty, spotted sheets, a tablecloth with a hole burned in its middle, other bedding items, and several other possessions that appeared totally worthless and unnecessary. She gave some of her prized belongings to the homeowners. Lenci and I just looked at each other with jaws hanging down in astonishment. We could not believe that Joe had carried these things so faithfully throughout our difficult journey!

# CHAPTER 17

# Journey to the U.S.A.

We planned to take a train for the continuation of our journey. The nearest train station was in another town which was quite a distance away. So that morning we set out for that town, with our host couple, using their cow-pulled buggy. The women and the children were seated in the buggy and the men walked alongside.

When we arrived at the station we said good-bye to Salty. We also departed from the couple who had crossed the border with us, and their baby. Morris went to buy our train tickets to Kecskemet, where Lenci had a sister in whose home we could stay. We boarded the train in the morning and traveled throughout that day. We fell asleep and when we woke up, we found that I had a relapse of the hepatitis. My skin and the whites of my eyes turned completely yellow. We arrived in Kecskemet on the twenty-ninth of December and spent a few days there, while Joe and Morris proceeded to travel to Budapest to inquire about the possibilities of continuing on to Israel or to the United States.

A few days later Lenci and I traveled to Budapest to join Morris and Joe. We began to plan our future on the basis of information we had received from the HIAS organization, which was the Jewish agency that undertook to develop connections and opportunities for Jews to escape from Hungary to Austria.

We realized that we needed to wait, so we rented a furnished apartment in the capital. Lenci and I ran the household while our husbands made inquiries and arrangements in pursuit of our plan. While waiting, we used the time to make ourselves some clothes and bought suitcases for the anticipated journey.

Finally the day arrived when HIAS had arranged for our departure and border-crossing to Austria. We boarded a bus which was to transport us, along with many other refugees, across the border. On the bus we met a couple with a small boy, and we made conversation. They learned from us that we had not been asked to pay for our passage and told us that they had been required to pay to be taken across. I explained to the woman that people who had money were asked to pay for their trip so that people like us, who did not have any money, could be taken along, and that we would repay HIAS as soon as we were able to do so. We felt that such payment would enable the organization to help other refugees in their quest for freedom. It also turned out that these people were "legitimate" Hungarians, holding the appropriate documents, whereas we had no legal status, which put us in great danger.

When we reached the border we could see the Russian sentries guarding the area. We were very tense and nervous and we wondered whether we would succeed in our passage. The bus driver went off to talk to the sentry and later returned to tell us that we would have to get off the bus and walk some distance on foot. We gathered our belongings and proceeded to walk across the border. Then another bus arrived from the Austrian side. We boarded it and took off.

That evening we arrived in Vienna. We were driven to the Rothschild Center where we stayed for three nights. It was a horrible place. Polish refugees had lived there for several years in their attempts to avoid a return to Poland. Their very lengthy temporary stay was extended because they were unable to go anywhere. They owned very little and all their possessions were confined to a few suitcases. The sanitary conditions were deplorable and sub-standard by any measure. The conditions were so bad that during the first night of our stay Lenci could not stop crying hysterically. We were able to arrange for her and her son, Gabie, to sleep in the hospital ward, where it was cleaner. They slept there for two more nights until we were able to leave and move on to Ebelsberg, which was near the town of Linz. Linz was jointly occupied by American and Russian military forces. There was a displaced persons (D.P.) camp in Ebelsberg, previously used by the Austrian military. We were able to obtain a room there, which we divided in two with a cardboard partition. Lenci, Morris and Gabie lived on one side while Joe and I lived on the other.

The camp was not far from Linz, and we were able to go to town by train whenever we wanted. We had to be very careful not to go any farther than the Linz station because that part of the town constituted the Russian zone. We heard of instances where people who had fallen asleep on the train and had entered the Russian-controlled area were never seen again. There was a great deal of political animosity between the Americans and the Russians, and our objective was to remain in the American-controlled zone.

While in the D.P. camp, awaiting the next leg of our journey, Joe and Morris played soccer with some of the Polish men. Joe held a job with the Joint Distribution Agency. One of the men with whom he worked and played ball was able to convince him and Morris that Israel was not a good destination for us because of the ongoing war there and because life there was very difficult. He suggested that if we had relatives in the United States, we should try to arrange, through HIAS, to join them instead of going to Israel. I had some family members in New York, whom I had never met. All I knew about them was their name. Morris inquired about the possibility of making the change in our plans, but the HIAS officials said that proof of the existence of such relatives was required. We needed someone to sponsor us, but I had no way of making contact with my relatives. Lenci had a cousin in Milwaukee to whom she had written in an attempt to have her vouch for us. At about the same time, Joe was recruited to play on an Italian soccer team. He was offered a large sum of money to move to Italy and join the team, but we could not even conceive of the possibility of giving up our dream of getting to America. Joe declined the offer and we continued to wait, praying and hoping to make the connection which would earn us passage to the United States. America represented a long-sought dream of untold opportunity and freedom.

Finally we heard from Lenci's cousin in Milwaukee, who had arranged with HIAS to formally sponsor us as immigrants, which would guarantee us passage to the United States and a legal status there. This act put our plans in motion, and we began to take care of the required paperwork and documentation.

We remained in the D.P. camp for more than nine months, as we waited for the completion of all the necessary arrangements. Finally, on October 1, 1949, we were taken to the port city of Bremerhaven, where we boarded the *General Muir*, a military ship which was to take us to our long-sought America.

The *General Muir* was a military ship, and we joined other passengers. The ship was not equipped with stabilizers and the entire trip was rather bumpy. The weather was bad and the ocean was very rough. We traveled from Bremerhaven past Great Britain, west towards the United States, but by the time we passed the British Isles everyone on board was suffering from seasickness. I remember people lying about on the floor everywhere. My young nephew, Gabie, was the only one who did not become ill, and he kept saying, "I'm hungry! I'm hungry!" But no one was healthy enough to attend to the boy and take him below deck to feed him.

While at the D.P. camp in Austria, Lenci and I had taken private English lessons and were able to understand and speak some English. On the ship one day, early after our departure when everyone was seasick, I saw an American woman who seemed well, compared to the others. She ate and smoked cigarettes and walked around looking quite fit and healthy, so I asked her how she managed to avoid being as ill as the rest of us. She told me, "Tomorrow morning get up and go to the dining room, even if you have to crawl all the way to get there. Force yourself to eat some hard-boiled eggs with lots of salt and pepper on them. That will keep your stomach from being upset." I followed her suggestion to the letter. She was right! I felt much better almost instantly. In fact, I was able to take Gabie down to eat as well. Since no one else took the woman's advice seriously, I was the only one in the family to feel well enough, enabling me to move around and help out as needed.

On the tenth of October, 1949, we arrived in New York harbor. Excited, we stood with the other passengers around the railing on the ship's deck, waiting to see the famous city skyline.

I had goose bumps all over my body as we saw New York from the ship, and I was choked with emotion at the sight of the Statue of Liberty. We saw our future. At last we had freedom and a new life.

# Epilogue

## New York

When we disembarked in New York, Lenci's niece, Ingrid, was waiting for us. She had gone to the HIAS office and formally took full responsibility for us. We went to her apartment, where we spent our first night in the United States. She promised to take us to the train station on the following day, to continue on to our destination, Milwaukee, Wisconsin. Our documents originated from Wisconsin so we had to travel to that city.

In her apartment that evening, I took the telephone book and began to look through it for the names of relatives. I knew that I had cousins in New York. We did discover the names of Joe's relatives including one aunt. Ingrid made the telephone calls for us and on that very night Joe's aunt came to visit us. She was an old lady who lived with her daughter. I also asked Ingrid to call many people named Friedlander, in my search for my relatives. One person who answered the call turned out to be my cousin and we were able to establish initial contact and to inform them of our destination and future location.

**Wisconsin**

On the next day we took the train to Milwaukee. HIAS had arranged for us to be put up in an apartment in a big house on Knapp Street. When we entered the living room in the two-bedroom apartment, we found a large bowl of fresh fruit on the table. I will never forget the sight of the huge bowl of bananas, oranges, apples, and other fruit. The thought has since then endured in my mind that the kindness of strangers can make a difference in people's lives. We had never before been the recipients of help from organizations such as HIAS. We were somewhat independent in our lives and we did not know much about the organization. Now we were learning to see a new way of life—people helping people. They brought us into a new world. They received us with an apartment, complete with towels and bedding, as well as butter and milk in the refrigerator. It was a new phenomenon for us! It brought a good, warm, feeling and we were very grateful!

HIAS also found us jobs. Lenci worked with her cousin at a meat-packing factory while Gabie, who was two years old, went to a nursery school. I had a job in a wood-working factory and later at a tannery. It was smelly and hard, but it was work. Joe and Morris worked in a machine shop. Joe came home every evening covered with grease. He had to scrape off the oil and take a long bath to clean up. But his job offered good income. We saved every penny that we could because we did not intend to stay in Milwaukee. Lenci had a sister and an aunt who lived in San Francisco and when we talked with them on the telephone they always said, "Don't buy anything because you're not going to remain there. You're going to move to California as soon as you have enough money and can let go of the HIAS security."

So all we did was work and save. We could not go until we had saved enough money. For us, HIAS offered security in many ways. Not only did they secure us an apartment and jobs, they also enrolled us in a health plan in a local hospital, which was very important.

Later, Lenci and I managed to obtain better positions at Frank's Sausage Factory. It was a good paying job but the working conditions were far from ideal. It was always very cold. In the summer, while the weather was extremely hot outside, the inside temperatures were at freezing level, like working inside a refrigerator. The room in which we worked was actually refrigerated. We had to weigh the cold cuts and then send them on to packaging. Later the factory was moved to Chicago and by that time we had saved enough money. The relocation of the factory provided us with a good reason to make our move to California.

All in all, we stayed in Milwaukee for almost a year. We did not like living there. The winter was very cold and the summer was too hot for us. The autumn, however, was beautiful. We were committed to staying in Milwaukee for two reasons. First, Joe and Morris had made a commitment to play for the local soccer team at least until the end of the season. They played in a televised game for twenty minutes every Sunday, as part of an Oldsmobile advertising promotion. Second, we were determined to save enough money to get us to California and to start our lives over, without relying on the help of HIAS.

The time to make the move arrived. We had worked hard, saved some money, and gave our apartment back to HIAS, including everything that we had received from them. Before moving, Joe and I bought a new Buick. I did not know how to drive, but Joe had taken a few driving classes in Austria and had obtained an international driver's license. He had not had any opportunities to practice his driving in the U.S., but he trained himself and practiced his skills before our departure. Lenci, Morris and Gabie were to travel to California by train and meet us there.

## California

We left for California on September 1, 1950. Joe had tried to teach me to drive the car, but I could not get the hang of it and Joe said, "Okay, you can't drive!" and that was the end of that! So, he drove by himself all the way west. We arrived in California on September 5. When we reached the Golden Gate bridge we were overwhelmed by the congestion. We had never before seen so many cars and so much traffic. We were somewhat intimidated.

We went directly to a hotel in San Francisco where arrangements had been made for us by the local Jewish soccer team, Hakkoah. They had recruited Joe and Morris while we were still in Milwaukee. Lenci's sister and her brother-in-law, Alex, made all the arrangements with officials of the team, who made it clear that they were very excited and eager to have the two on their team. They helped us find jobs and helped us settle in. Joe and I moved into an apartment on Geary Boulevard. Lenci, Morris and Gabie moved in with Lenci's sister, to a large and beautifully furnished Mission Street apartment. Morris and Joe began to work in a shoe store on the San Francisco peninsula. Later, Joe and I moved to a nice studio apartment on Minna Street.

I started to work in Benetar's Drug Store in the city. Since the holiday season and Christmas were approaching, my duty was to giftwrap. This was a temporary seasonal position and I was to lose the job after the holidays. I was a hard worker and I had established a friendly relationship with the owner's daughter, so I remained employed until

March of the following year, when they were forced to let me go because there was no more work for me to do.

My next job was at Moore's Cafeteria. My English was still rather poor and I was not able to take on responsibilities other than bussing tables. It was better than staying at home and it provided an income. Within a few weeks, I befriended my boss who, it turned out, was a Hungarian American. We conversed through his broken Hungarian and my poor English. I asked for a better position and he asked me if I could count and work with figures. I said, "Sure!" He tried me out as a checker. I had to hand the people waiting in line a ticket for whatever they selected to buy and add on three percent for the sales tax. When he discovered that I was able to carry out the responsibility without any problems, he promoted me to a cashier's position. This was a much better job because I was able to sit down and it was much easier on my feet. I was happy with this job and I kept it for three years.

We had applied for American citizenship as soon as we could. We were so anxious to become "real" U.S. citizens that we had asked our landlord in Milwaukee to sign the needed documents for us so that the short time that we had spent in Milwaukee would be calculated toward the required five-year waiting period. We became citizens in 1954 and it was one of the happiest days of our lives.

With time we saved enough money to buy our first house, in the town of Millbrae. We did not have enough money for furniture, and my brother Eddie sent me five hundred dollars. I also obtained a bank loan for another five hundred dollars, and we used the money to buy a bedroom set, a table, chairs and a small radio receiver. Once again we felt that life was good for us. We worked hard and began repaying our debt to HIAS. Every month we sent a check to cover the costs of delivering us from Austria. Once the loan was paid off, we continued to make regular contributions to HIAS, as a show of our gratitude and appreciation for what they had done for us and for others.

After being employed for a year in the shoe store, Joe and Morris left their jobs and, with Lenci's brother-in-law, Alex Smook, pooled their money and opened their own shoe store in Millbrae. They bought an inexpensive Chevrolet which they drove all the way back east to buy merchandise for their new venture.

The store was successful from the very beginning, but we did not use the income for personal purposes. The most important thing for us was the establishment of a solid business foundation. So we invested most of our profits in the shoe store, using the revenues to buy quality merchandise and build up the business. Our language skill had improved significantly with time and Lenci was able to secure a good job as a teller in a local branch of the Bank of America. Helen Smook, Lenci's sister, was employed as a drape-maker at the City of Paris store, and I worked as a cashier at Moore's Cafeteria. In this way, the women supported the families, providing for the ongoing expenses and needs, while the men used the fruits of their labor to build up the business.

Meanwhile, Joe and I were still trying to have a baby, but after about thirteen years we became discouraged and arranged to adopt a child. The details were arranged through a Jewish agency that found us a year-and-a-half-old boy who suffered from heart trouble. He was to undergo surgery, the cost of which was to be covered by the agency. He desperately needed a loving family. It was arranged for us to meet the boy's mother, a divorced woman with another, older, child. Before we had a chance to meet the woman, she changed her mind and decided to keep the boy.

Later we became aware of another possibility: a woman who was carrying the child of an "old flame," while she was divorced, raising a ten-year-old child and a twenty-year-old who was away in college. She had decided to put up the expected baby for adoption. We met the woman and she liked us. She agreed to the adoption and the process was under way after we made a $550 deposit to cover the mother's hospital costs. While waiting for the birth, I discovered that I was pregnant! We decided to go ahead with the adoption anyway, but the expectant mother changed her mind and decided to keep her baby. On November 19, 1958, at the age of thirty-eight, I gave birth to our baby girl, Amber. Nothing matched the happiness we felt to finally have the baby that we wanted for so long!

Earlier that year, Joe's brother Alex and his wife Hanna had joined us in California. They had escaped from Romania before we did and had been living in New York City for a while.

The shoe store in Millbrae was doing very well and we opened another one in the city of Sunnyvale, to the south, where Alex and Hanna had settled. Joe trained them and taught them the shoe business, about which they had no knowledge or experience. For about a year, Joe drove to Sunnyvale almost daily to work with them. They were good learners and were able to put into work and practice what they had been taught. The business thrived and we were all partners: Lenci and Morris, Alex and Helen, Alex and Hanna, and Joe and I.

Earlier in 1956, following the uprising and upheaval in Hungary, Lenci's other sister, Bobbie, and her husband, Emmanuel, managed to escape with their daughter, Judy. They, too, made their way to California. They spoke no

English, but Bobbie, too, was offered a job at Moore's Cafeteria, upon my recommendation. Emmanuel began to work in one of the shoe stores. Later on, they, too, joined the partnership and with our help opened another shoe store in San Carlos. We had built up interest in three shoe stores, and business was very good.

With time, the women of the family left their jobs to join the work force in the shoe stores. By the beginning of the 1960s we earned enough of a profit to live on without needing to engage in outside work. In 1961 we sold our house in Millbrae and bought the home in which we currently live, in Burlingame, just south of Millbrae. We lived comfortably and happily off the income from the shoe stores and have always invested and put aside money for the future.

In 1961 we traveled out of the country for the first time, as proud American passport holders. We went to Israel to visit my sister Miriam, her daughter Irene and their families. Following their escape, Irene got married in the town of Kolosvar and with her husband, Tibi, lived in Oradea. They moved to Israel when their firstborn son, Chaim, was seven months old, in 1949, and had lived there since. Miriam, too, was remarried. We also saw my brother, Nathan, whom I had not seen since we lived in Satu-Mare, before the war.

We also had an opportunity to go back to Budapest where I visited my sister Lenke, who had come there from Bucharest, with her husband. Our trip took place during the Stalin era, and it was quite frightening to return behind the iron curtain. But we had our American passports. We knew that we were safe with our American citizenship, and we felt that the world was ours.

## Today

Throughout her youth, my daughter knew that I had been in a concentration camp and that we had escaped from behind the iron curtain. We told her about our past as early as she was able to comprehend such matters. She did not know the details, however, until she was in high school. One day her teacher asked me to speak to her social studies class about my experiences, as they were studying World War II.

After I spoke to her class, my daughter hugged and kissed me and said, "Mom, why didn't you ever talk about this before? Why didn't you ever tell me about all of this?" I explained to her that her father did not want me to talk about the bad times because he felt that we should focus on the present and on our future rather than on the past. Besides, it just never seemed to be the right time to bring up the story. Now I realize that we should have talked about those years and about our fate, so that it will never be forgotten and history will never repeat itself. There are valuable lessons to be learned from our experiences and they should not remain sealed in our subconscious.

Following my appearances in the schools I was asked many times to return and retell the story in many social studies classes, which I did, without ever refusing. Word got around and I was invited many more times to talk to students in different schools. I feel that I am on a mission, in a sense, trying to preserve the memories and to help protect the world from another holocaust.

When I speak to high school students in the San Francisco Bay Area, students often ask, "Do you hate the Germans?" At first I had to think about the question for a while, for I was not certain. Now I always answer, "No, I don't hate them. I can't hate a nation. If I did, I would not be any better than the Nazis were. I don't have hate in my heart. You see," I tell them, "even after my terrible ordeal I can't hate anyone. Even though I could hate the persons who had committed the atrocities, I couldn't seek revenge. I feel that the punishment is in the hands of the appropriate authorities. It's not for me to do. I leave it in the hands of God."

One student's remark stays in my mind. He said, "I don't understand why the Nazis would want you killed. You don't look any different from my grandmother." I replied, "Doesn't that tell you something?"

Our daughter had graduated from Mills High School in Millbrae in 1976 and went on to attend the University of Southern California in Los Angeles. She earned her bachelor's degree in fine arts and later attended San Francisco State University, where she received her master's degree in education along with teaching credentials. She was a high school teacher in the Bay Area. She is the mother of a lovely daughter, Kailei, whom we adore. Kailei, a very bright and beautiful girl, spends the night with us, in our home, about once every week and she is a joy to have around. My daughter is also an artist and a musician, playing the saxophone professionally with her own band. Presently she is a librarian in a local high school.

I believe in God, and I keep the Jewish faith and Jewish tradition, although I do not consider myself to be a religious person. I raised my daughter in a Jewish household but she did not remain Jewish in her spiritual beliefs. She does consider herself Jewish, though, through birth. One thing that I had always tried to teach her was to be a good, moral person. I succeeded at that, and although we went through some difficult times during her adolescence, she grew up to be a person of good character that we can be proud of. I know she is trying to instill the same beliefs and values in our granddaughter. She does not raise her to be a religious Jew, but she tells Kailei that she is Jewish by birth and that she will always remain Jewish no matter what she believes spiritually.

Very often I have nightmares which take me back to the terrible experiences I endured. For some reason, in my dreams I am always in hiding and frequently protecting a child. Perhaps it is because I have a daughter and a granddaughter and I worry about their futures. I always wake up terrified as I dream of being shot to death. This dream recurs often even though it has been more than fifty years since the holocaust. I can never forget it. Sometimes I wish that I could forget, but there is not one day in my life without recurring visions, memories, and feelings from the past.

The Nazis systematically stripped us of our dignity, rightful existence, freedom, citizenship and, ultimately, of our lives, in the most cruel and heartless manner. We were forced to endure the unbelievable sight of our loved ones being tortured and killed right before our very eyes, knowing that our own fate could be the same or worse. Mothers and fathers with children of all ages had to stand around for long hours, naked and desperate, hungry, cold, embarrassed and humiliated. All this pain and suffering was inflicted upon us for no other reason than having been born an unfavorable religion in the Nazi's estimation. Because of this, a madman's followers were given the right to live out their sadistic fantasies as a reality, with live victims of their choice. As I look back at the unjust history of pain and suffering that has been inflicted upon the Jews, I find myself still amazed. Who would have thought that the world could allow this to happen in the twentieth century? It is my wish that by putting these experiences down on paper, I would help bring the awareness necessary for future generations to prevent this kind of tragedy from happening again.

Now we are happily retired, and able to enjoy the fruits of all our labor. Somehow, after all the hardships we endured, I think that we can appreciate life even more than ever before. We know how bad it can be and that contrast serves to make our lives that much sweeter now. Some people dwell on the small problems that occur in their daily existence, not realizing how bad things can really be. Once a person has experienced the extreme traumas that I have, the small problems that life can dish out seem so insignificant. It has served as the utmost contrast in my life, making me a very happy person, grateful for even those small problems. When I awake every morning, I realize that I am grateful just to be alive and see the shining sun.

I have often been asked by students to what I attribute my survival where so many have perished. My answer is that my survival is attributable to the grace of God, my positive attitude, and sheer luck. No matter how hopeless and terrible our suffering was, I continually told those around me who had lost all hope to hold on, that there would be a rest period soon, that there is a tomorrow, that freedom will come, and that the genocide will end. Now, as a free person, I fear that it could happen again. This fear always brings to my mind the warning that if people forget the lessons of history, they might repeat the same mistakes. For this reason, I take every opportunity I can to speak out in high schools and university classes, to tell my story and to make certain that it is remembered.